D0844736

DATE DUE

BRODART, CO.

Cat. No. 23-221

Understanding Sharks

Understanding Sharks

The Fascinating Behavior
of a Threatened Hunter

Erich Ritter

KRIEGER PUBLISHING COMPANY
Malabar, Florida
2006

With 221 color photographs and 13 color figures.
Cover by eStudio Calamar, Pau, created by combining two color photographs by Bernd Humberg (Diver) and SHARKPROJECT (Shark).

Original German Edition *Mit Haien sprechen* 2004
Original English Edition 2006

Printed and Published by
KRIEGER PUBLISHING COMPANY
KRIEGER DRIVE
MALABAR, FLORIDA 32950

Copyright © German Edition 2004 by Franckh-Kosmos Verlags-GmbH & Co.KG, Stuttgart, Germany.
Copyright © English Edition 2006 by Krieger Publishing Company
Translated from the original German by Valerie Haecky

All rights reserved. No part of this book may be reproduced in any form or by any means, electronic or mechanical, including information storage and retrieval systems without permission in writing from the publisher.
No liability is assumed with respect to the use of the information contained herein.

Printed in China.

FROM A DECLARATION OF PRINCIPLES JOINTLY ADOPTED BY A COMMITTEE OF THE AMERICAN BAR ASSOCIATION AND A COMMITTEE OF PUBLISHERS:
This publication is designed to provide accurate and authoritative information in regard to the subject matter covered. It is sold with the understanding that the publisher is not engaged in rendering legal, accounting, or other professional service. If legal advice or other expert assistance is required, the services of a competent professional person should be sought.

Library of Congress Cataloging-in-Publication Data

Ritter, Erich (Erich Kurt)
   [Mit Haien sprechen. English]
   Understanding sharks : the fascinating behavior of a threatened hunter / Erich Ritter ;
   [translated from the original German by Valerie Haecky].
       p. cm.
   Includes bibliographical references (p.) and index.
   ISBN 1-57524-269-9 (alk. paper)
   1. Sharks—Behavior. I. Title.
   QL638.9R57 2006
   597.3'15—dc22
                                                         2005044420

       10 9 8 7 6 5 4 3 2

ACC LIBRARY SERVICES
AUSTIN, TX

For my parents—
their support over many years has made it all possible.

Contents

Foreword

Unappreciated Animals Need Acknowledgment and Sympathy

We know little about sharks and their biology, and even less about their behavior. Therefore, studies and reports about them are all too easily distorted by the many myths, legends, and exaggerated stories in the media.

We are not aware that there are a large variety of sharks, because only the relatively few large and spectacular species are at the center of our interest, while at the same time most of the other species are ignored. The obsession of people, newspapers, television, and even some scientists with shark attacks and the related selachophobia—that is, the fear of sharks—are significant obstacles towards a true understanding of these animals. Negative, overly emotional, and anthropocentric, this preoccupation with shark attacks covers up the reality that a person being injured by a shark is a rare event. Fear of these animals, and the search for answers in a state of fear and disgust, lead to subjective judgments that only confirm our fears and make objective research difficult. In addition, there is a strong tendency by the public and scientists, to attach negative human characteristics to sharks and condemn them as evil. All these factors contribute to disregard for, persecution of, and ultimately possible extirpation of these animals.

Sharks are usually studied from the point of view of their economic value and use, but recently—fortunately—also from the realization that they are close to extinction and something must be done to protect them. However, this has resulted in more research of only a few species, while most others are completely ignored or only studied in passing. So far, the importance of sharks for the ecology of the oceans has hardly been researched. Only slowly are we beginning to gain first insights into shark sociobiology, behaviors, or ecology of behavior. Certainly, it is more difficult to research the life of sharks than that of terrestrial vertebrates—but it is possible, as this book demonstrates.

The book presented here by Dr. Erich Ritter, is fundamentally different from other books about sharks. It inspires rethinking, since it goes beyond the general views about sharks and the often narrow thinking that permeates current shark research. The book integrates studies of the shark-human relationship into the behavioral research of sharks, and substantiates this through ongoing field research with the large species that are often involved in accidents. A primary theme in this book is the fear of sharks, and the book shows that interactions between sharks and humans are one way towards overcoming this fear. This requires understanding of the complex behaviors of both humans and sharks. This book also gives a clear message on the necessity for shark conservation, and it suggests that sharks really have good reason to be more afraid of us than we are of them, if only they knew more about us.

A famous ichthyologist once wrote a paper with the title "Are We on the Right Track with Sharks." He found no convincing answer—but his question remains and can now be answered with a clear "No!" We are NOT on the right track, as long as the fear of sharks dominates our thinking. We need comprehensive studies on shark biology in order to better understand their world, their ecological value, and our impact on them—and we need it before sharks disappear from this planet. This is not about controlled management of shark populations, which worldwide really doesn't exist anyway. This is about a fundamental understanding of sharks and their right to exist.

This book attempts to create understanding and sympathy for these fascinating animals. It demonstrates the complexity of shark behaviors, the shark-human relationship, and the current endangerment of this group of animals, and it helps us find the proper way of dealing with sharks and ourselves.

Dr. Leonard J.V. Compagno
Head of Shark Research Center,
South African Museum

Why It Is Important to Know, Understand, and Respect Sharks

Sharks are amazing animals, beautiful and mysterious at the same time. They awaken our anger and captivate our hearts. We fear them, and at the same time are also fascinated by them. Even though the opposite is always asserted, we still know very little about the behavior of these incredible animals.

In this wonderful book by Erich Ritter, we get to learn about shark behavior, for example, how do sharks react to various stimuli from their environment. The more we learn about the true character of these animals, the more we must come to accept that they are not the aggressive monsters for which they are often taken.

Quite the opposite is the case: if we take the time to study the behaviors and body language of sharks, we also learn about unknown aspects of their lives. If we give them some of our time to explain themselves, we will quickly notice that we are not doing them justice by representing them as cruel man-eaters that attack everything and everybody they encounter. In fact, most situations where sharks become dangerous are created by us.

I particularly appreciate that this book emphasizes how important it is to observe these animals in the footsteps of the classic behavioral scientists Konrad

Lorenz and Niko Tinbergen. I especially like the captions that accompany the numerous photographs: Why do sharks lower their pectoral fins, why do they twist their bodies in certain situations, why do they gape, why do they yawn, why do they circle around a person? The answers to these and many other questions are of incredible value to all of us. The text and figures in this book certainly contribute to changing our ideas about sharks, which are greatly influenced by myths. Many misunderstandings that are held up by books written for entertainment create completely unnecessary hatred towards sharks without our knowing the animals at all. Knowledge leads us to understanding. Understanding helps us recognize the value of things and living beings, and valuing leads to respect.

This book accomplishes something additional: It encourages readers to consider the "big" questions of human existence. And it shows us that we must cease to exploit Nature towards our own ends. Because, in the final reckoning, we will have to suffer the consequences.

Many species of animals are in a precarious state. On one hand, they are used and exploited by humans, on the other hand, venerated and appreciated. Animals contribute significantly to our well-being, a fact of which most people are unaware. Therefore, a special mission is manifesting itself: We all must take care of the Earth and its inhabitants. If we practice consideration and respect towards all living beings on this planet, all animals, humans, plants, and habitats, we will do considerably better than would be the case without peaceful cohabitation, respect, caring, compassion, humility, generosity, benevolence, mercy, and love. In fact, it is like this: If we take care of our environment, we also take care of ourselves. Our souls have been damaged by our estrangement from the natural world of animals and other living beings. Those who choose once more to live in connection and harmony with Nature can realize their true selves, discover new wonders, find their hidden dreams, and bring them to life.

We require animals, plants, the natural world, and wilderness! Without them we cannot exist! For our own benefit, we must understand sharks and other animals, and actively protect them to save them from extirpation. If they should disappear from our Earth, we would painfully miss them.

Mark Bekoff
Professor of Environmental, Population, and Organism Biology at the University of Colorado at Boulder, Colorado

How It All Began…

My lifelong fascination with sharks was what brought me to Walker's Cay, Bahamas, in April of 2002; and of course, the stories of my friend Andy Cobb, who raved about Dr. Ritter and his experiments for a long time in South Africa. I wanted to meet this Dr. Erich Ritter, and of course I also wanted to interact with "his" bull sharks. I encountered a fascinating person, shy and reserved, unless the topic was his animals, when he was carried off by contagious enthusiasm. We spent an endless evening at a bar, where we built the foundation for a very long friendship that would further develop during the following fateful months. By the end of this first evening, the conclusion to draw from our discussion was evident to both of us: sharks are not soulless, man-eating monsters, but to the contrary, like all other predators, very shy, restrained animals, for which humans are in no way a part of the natural diet. It is urgent that we protect these animals! But the enormous prejudice against sharks stands in the way of any conservation measures. Nobody protects something that they fear. It is therefore necessary, as a first step, to produce an advocate for these animals—

people who want to know and understand their world better.

Admittedly, everybody is familiar with these kinds of bar conversations, meant very seriously, but then when one returns to everyday life, the ideas get suffocated by everyday life demands and priorities.

Maybe our idea for a shark protection lobby would have met the same fate if there had not been an accident in the morning of the next day. During a television interview among sharks, one animal bit Dr. Ritter in the calf—the consequence of a chain of unfortunate circumstances. He lost a lot of blood, was immediately transported to Miami, and for the next weeks and months was suspended between death and amputation.

This period of time was used by many scientific colleagues and reporters to aggressively debunk the myth of the "Shark Whisperer." The accident was fuel for the fire for his enemies. Anybody who represents a position that is contrary to the generally accepted opinion has enemies—we all know this. During this time the "Jetzt-erst-recht" (trans. "Now-more-than-ever") movement came into existence. Many e-mails, phone calls, and personal meetings followed, and SHARKPROJECT became a reality. In September of 2002, together with other scientists, environmentalists, divers, and shark sympathizers, we founded an international initiative for the protection of and research on sharks. Its foundation: that original late night conversation at the bar in Walker's Cay. All our ideas, how we could protect and research sharks, are now part of the concept of this initiative. Only one year later—SHARKPROJECT e.V. was one of the largest shark conservation organizations in the world, and certainly the most dynamic one. Over 300,000 people have visited our web site (www.sharkproject.com) in the last 12 months, and over 7000 people have listened to our shark talks in Germany, Austria, and Switzerland. First film contributions have been created, and many experiments and research activities have taken place.

The most important task remains today: How can we reduce the prejudice against sharks? We do not understand them—and that creates fear in us. This fear can be dissipated, if we understand shark body language and can interpret it in the same ways as for an unknown dog that we would not fear, since we know what the animal is telling us with its body language. This is what this book is about. With many examples of interactions and research results from Dr. Ritter, we learn to understand sharks and properly assess their behavior.

What remains is a respect and fascination for one of the most misunderstood living beings on this planet. That creates a foundation for the urgent protection of these animals, because worldwide it is already less than one second before midnight. More than 200 million sharks are killed annually by humans, and many shark species are at the brink of extinction. It is high time for a book like this one!

As publishers of this book, we are happy to make another important contribution towards the protection of sharks.

Gerhard Wegner
President SHARKPROJECT e.V.
International Initiative for the Protection and Research on Sharks e.V.

Preface

In recent years, many books about sharks have been published, and all of them discuss the same topics, namely, how sharks attack, behave, hunt, eat, and reproduce. None of the information was questioned, but always copied from previous authors, sometimes illustrated with new photographs, but essentially remaining the same. This book does not follow in the same old footsteps, but presents these ocean inhabitants from a different perspective.

This book clarifies that sharks are not the stereotypical machines as which they are still often portrayed in films and articles. Sharks—just like other animals—encounter a variety of problems in their daily lives. They deal with them sometimes more and sometimes less successfully. Like other, more familiar animals, sharks are in the final analysis, only animals that are adapted to their habitat and their role in the larger context of the natural world.

This book describes the behavior of these animals in their natural habitat as well as towards members of the same species and toward humans. It includes new data about the behavior of sharks. It provides general background information in order to make it easier to understand the data. Topics such as reproduction or senses are only mentioned in passing and only explained in so far as they are significant in the context of shark behavior and its classification in a larger context.

Worldwide, humans kill 200 million sharks annually—partly out of indifference, partly out of greed or fear. This killing based on "questionable motives" has the result that many shark species are threatened with extinction, and that our generation will probably be the last one to see and experience representatives of many shark species. This is even more disastrous, because the natural world requires sharks! Without these predators at the top of the marine food chains, the oceanic ecosystem will collapse. Since humans can only survive in an intact environment, of which a healthy ocean is a mandatory component, we humans require sharks! It is therefore in our most basic interest to immediately put a stop to the current worldwide mass destruction of sharks! The situation looks even more dire when one realizes that sharks, unlike other bony fish, reproduce extremely slowly, and once a population has been decimated, it is rarely able to recover. Once most of these large predators have been destroyed and lost to the ocean ecosystem, the marine food chains will collapse with unpredictable consequences also for humans!

It is the intention of this book to reduce the fear that many readers have of sharks by providing detailed information about their behavior, and to transform the general indifference into an active interest in these fascinating living beings. Sharks must be brought closer to the heart of the general public! It is finally time to dispel the myth of the monster shark. Fear of sharks is inappropriate—none of these animals bites blindly or randomly attacks any person within reach. Sharks have the same right to live and are equally worthy of protection as all other animals. Especially in terms of financial resources, their protection must be worth as much as that of other species of animals. Sharks urgently need a strong lobby. If successive generations are to be able to experience these animals, we must fight for that immediately. Sharks are fascinating, but unfortunately still misunderstood. This book is a contribution to changing that.

Acknowledgments

My biggest thanks go to Gerhard Wegner, President of SHARKPROJECT—closest friend and visionary. His energy, help, and words of support have made this book possible. I also thank his wife Christel, who took over many administrative tasks and listened to me whenever I got stuck. Special thanks also go to Christine Staacks, the webmaster for SHARKPROJECT, for the many improvements to the figures.

This book is based on many conversations. I would like to thank all who answered my questions, whose views I often questioned, or with whom I discussed issues and explored new venues: as representatives for all, I give thanks to Leonard Compagno and André Hartmann.

Page xviii/1:
A great white shark displays RAG (Repetitive Aerial Gaping): The animal is swimming at the surface and opening and closing its mouth relatively slowly. Interpretations of this behavior range from frustration to expectation.

Encountering
Sharks

Sharks are mostly depicted with their mouths wide open. This behavior is only typical for great white sharks.

Fear of Sharks

Sharks trigger fear and revulsion in humans, as well as fascination and respect, like no other species of animal. They are the symbol of "angstination"—a word of my own creation made up of "angst" and "fascination": humans are afraid of sharks and at the same time feel magically attracted to them. No other animal radiates so much strength and elegance but also apparent danger and primitiveness.

Especially in Western civilization the fear of sharks is very pronounced. It is one reason why in a comparatively short period of time a large number of these ocean inhabitants will have disappeared from the planet forever.

Sharks are exposed to the negative emotions of most people without protection. And this, even though on some Pacific islands they are revered by people as gods, and it is documented that sharks are not the initiators of the small number of annual shark accidents. Neither this fact nor the knowledge that the existence of many shark species is threatened moves Western civilized nations towards the insight that something must be done to stop the senseless killing and wasting of sharks.

In order to effectively protect sharks, it must first be understood why there is fear of sharks to begin with and where it originates. Is it the appearance of the animal? Is it the environment? Is it the way in which a shark approaches? Or does this animal simply appear threatening to humans because it lives in a foreign medium? Probably all these factors put together are what makes it impossible for most people to see anything other than a terrible monster when they see a shark. However, one aspect seems particularly important.

When examining pictures and writings about sharks over the last decades, one thing is strikingly apparent: Photographs and movies show the shark always as an animal that can in no way be categorized. One cannot determine what it thinks, what its intentions are, what its gestures mean when it approaches or when it is accidentally encountered. One cannot

"read" the shark, that is, determine from visual clues what it wants and what mood it is in.

Especially this inability to interpret and understand sharks has led people to be afraid of them. Let us, for example, look at cats or dogs. The moods and

A highpoint for every sport diver: Sharks.

Typical behavior during commercial open ocean fishing: Sharks' fins are cut off for making shark fin soup.

intentions of these animals are revealed to us through their facial expressions and their body language in a familiar way, so that we are rarely afraid of them. However, even in human-to-human meetings, if someone talks to us in a foreign language, it often seems intimidating because of their different language and their unfamiliar facial expressions and gestures. The same is true for sharks. Therefore, I show in this book that sharks also have a body language and that it is possible to interact and communicate with them.

I often use the term "interacting at the same level" when describing meetings of humans with sharks. For me this term means that human and shark meet in an open-minded way, where persons do not put themselves above the shark, but also do not allow themselves to be influenced by myths. A person that interacts with a shark on the same level tries to find common ground, so that both can get to know each other without aggression. When two beings interact, they notice each other and mutually influence each other's behavior.

Managing Fear of Sharks

We are all afraid of a variety of things and situations. Well-founded fear—such as of lightning—is necessary, because it protects us from accidents and makes us act carefully and consider the consequences. Fear can also be unfounded and only arise in our heads. Then it prevents us from being truly free and can develop into life-limiting and hostile phobias. To increase our degree of freedom and act differently from before, we often would like to overcome our fears. But very often the fear is too great and the obstacle seems too big to overcome. Sharks, too, seem to trigger fear in many people, and that, even though most people have never encountered a shark.

I tend to think that this fear is created and kept alive by the media and a flood of false information. I suspect this even more, when I make encounters between sharks and humans possible in my courses and often

observe how quickly this apparent fear turns into fascination.

Only rarely have I met a person in one of my shark school courses (see p. 251) whom I could not convince

An object is inside the "inner circle" of this blacktip reef shark. The way in which it is turning its body to the right indicates that it will swim off to the right (animal's viewpoint).

Bull sharks have a very small individual space ("inner circle"). This is why they approach an object closely and turn away relatively late.

that fear of sharks is unfounded. It always is or was the humans that (knowingly or unknowingly, as for example, sport fishermen standing next to a bathing person) created the dangerous situation with sharks.

When I lead people towards sharks, it is often like behavioral therapy, in that I lead the people not only towards their own perceived fear, but also allow them to handle their fear on their own. Of course, people can also be convinced by logic and theories. But experience shows that fear can only be overcome permanently, and in a way that manifests itself in daily life, if the object of the fear has not only been heard about and seen, but also been felt and experienced.

I receive interesting answers when I ask people when their fear turned into fascination (see "Angstination", p. 3). Most of them say that it happened when they became aware that a shark was in front of them and it did not (!), as expected, approach and bite them. What happened in reality was exactly the opposite of what they expected, and exactly this expectation is what I use as a key factor in overcoming fears. If one really did

expect to be bitten, who would enter the water? Probably
nobody. It is just this confused way of thinking that
indicates to me that one cannot really be convinced
that the fear of sharks is unfounded in reality since
the rational part of the mind is completely convinced
of the danger.

How Can Fear of Sharks Be Overcome?

I am first interested in finding out where the persons to be convinced stand in respect to diving, water, and general well-being in their surroundings, in everyday life etc. This gives me the first hints as to their nervousness (N) and experience (Exp) and also helps me choose the environment (Env) in which to stage their first encounter with sharks. Since nervousness is influenced by a variety of factors (see also ADORE-SANE, p. 122), my first goal must be to be make the person aware of these factors and explain as many of them as possible. Only when I know that the persons are capable of handling themselves—as if they were spectators observing their problem on a stage without interacting—do I also know that I will be able to create a first positive interaction with sharks. At this first contact, the person is only a spectator and not doing anything. This first contact is the first step to overcoming fear of sharks.

Once individuals have experienced this first contact, I start to explain the basics of shark body language and guide them towards an interaction. In order to accomplish this, it is important that the assumption that sharks are animals with which interaction is not possible, which cannot be understood, and with which a relationship cannot be established and developed, must be abandoned. This first interaction is the beginning of phase 2. From then on, it is left to the person how far they wish to delve into human-shark interaction. In most cases my guidance becomes unnecessary, because the participants begin to explore their own fascination and approach the animals or allow the situation to affect them.

Protecting Sharks—Why?

In addition to our fear of sharks, it is primarily our indifference towards them that is responsible for the fact that daily—without a worldwide outcry of

In the eyes of many people, sharks have no right to live and are considered only as merchandise.

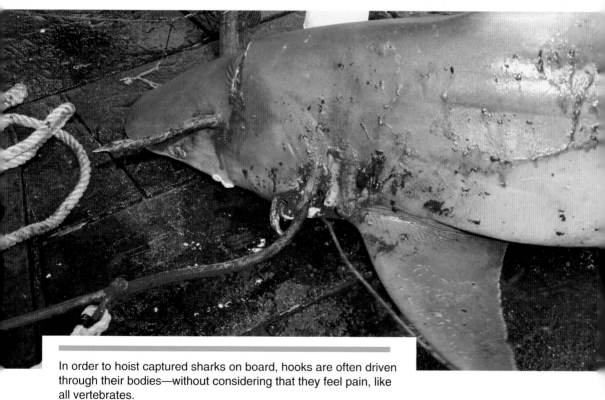

In order to hoist captured sharks on board, hooks are often driven through their bodies—without considering that they feel pain, like all vertebrates.

horror—hundreds of thousands of them are beaten to death, shot, slaughtered, or cut open. In my opinion, this outcry will finally be silenced when the largest ecological time bomb of all times—overfishing of sharks—explodes. Sharks are at the top of the marine ecosystem. Here they fulfill an ecologically important role, because they control the marine food chains and take injured, old, or sick animals out of circulation. In nature, everything is directly or indirectly interconnected. The elimination or decimation of one species can have unanticipated consequences for the others and trigger chain-reactions that cannot be stopped. For the ecological reasons alone, it is fatal to indifferently watch the extirpation of the most important marine predator.

The marine ecosystem will collapse if sharks cannot fulfill their task anymore.

Many scientists have recognized these problems for a long time; knowledge about the interplay of predators and prey in the ocean did not just arise yesterday. But obviously, these insights are still too abstract to motivate anyone to seriously take action to prevent this impending disaster. Sharks do not have a strong lobby fighting for them against overfishing, finning (cutting the fins off live sharks to produce shark fin soup), or the negative image that sensational movies spread. Can something be done against this exploitation? Yes, of course—it is not too late yet! But in order to succeed, action has to be taken immediately, and everybody has to help.

Learning to Understand Animals

Understanding the natural world requires studying and understanding the connections between animals and plants, as well as predators and prey, within an ecosystem. It is necessary to recognize the consequences that follow when the structure of relationships is changed or building blocks are destroyed. When animals and humans interact on the same level, we can understand them. These animals lose their status of anonymity—they become individuals. Some species of animals, however, have little chance of escaping this anonymity. Their only hope is that someone succeeds in elevating one or another representative of their species from anonymity and individualizes it. This often has the consequence that other members of the same species— at least by some people—are not seen as nameless masses anymore.

Anonymity means to me that an animal is not considered as an individual but as part of an amorphous group. It does not matter, whether this animal is a tiger shark, a blue shark, or a shark of another species—the only thing that matters is that it is a shark. With this attitude, all sharks are measured with the same measure and considered equal. The effect of loss of anonymity is that an animal will slowly be "understood" better. There is probably no dog owner who does not know how to interpret the basic body language of his or her dog. Owners have learned from books and from spending time with their dogs how to do this. However, interpreting a body movement, a way of approaching, or a characteristic posture is not accomplished overnight, but only through an ongoing process of learning. This process can only take place if the animal is given a certain amount of time to "blossom" and to communicate. Without this opportunity, a dog would never have become an individual in the past, and all the other members of its species would have remained unknown and misunderstood beings. Applying this to sharks shows exactly where one big problem lies.

In the last few years, hardly a person would want to spend more time with sharks than absolutely necessary; hardly anybody would give these animals the time necessary for them to "explain" themselves. Time and interest are required if sharks are to be understood as well as we understand dogs or cats.

Developing Observation Skills

My dog Bogy: Ideas for interacting with sharks first came to me while interacting with him.

The most important requirements for observing sharks or other animals are sufficient time and patience, so that the animals can reveal themselves and show their whole spectrum of behaviors.

Observing, however, does not mean just looking. One must learn to understand the patterns of what is seen, to interpret what is observed, and to compare it with previous observations. This makes evident one of the biggest problems concerning sharks. Apart from scuba divers and people who have discovered their fascination with sharks, most people will immediately leave the water when they see a shark, and they will do everything they can to make this first encounter their last one.

Without repeated observations and verifications, any first impressions and their interpretations remain hypothetical and most of the time no more than a mixture of fantasy and hearsay. In this way, sharks—or any other animal—cannot be understood properly or completely.

I know myself how important it is to repeatedly observe animals precisely. I recall clearly the first situation after I brought my new dog Bogy home from the shelter. I was sitting on a chair and he was sitting on the couch. What he wanted to tell me with his body language was a mystery to me at the time. Only much later I had learned to understand his actions through much observation and experience, and I understood that Bogy had not wanted to sit on the couch, but had jumped up there to signal that he wanted to be let outside. Only after I had seen this behavior several times, did I learn to interpret it accurately. Understanding of my dog increased, because I had him with me constantly and gave him time to "explain" himself.

Once more: Exactly this kind of time must be given to sharks if they are to be understood, and the core

A great white shark is
encouraged to bite.

learning consists in analyzing and understanding
shark body language.

In order for this learning to be successful, one must
first interact with these animals, observe them, and
critically question whether any interpretations of
what is seen is consistent with the facts. If the answer
is yes, it must be verified through experiments. If the
latter do not produce conclusive results, one has to
start over with more observation.

Pages 18/19:
Sand tiger sharks
actively swallow air to
increase buoyancy.

Shark Body Language and Behavior

How Sharks Perceive Their Environment

Before specific behaviors of sharks can be discussed, the sense organs of sharks must first be explained. Like every other living being, sharks have a number of sense organs. During an encounter with a shark, one may notice its seemingly unmoving eyes or believe that one has been smelled or heard. Because this is an anthropocentric interpretation where one draws conclusions about the shark based on experience with one's own body, one never knows for sure, which senses the shark is actually using and how it perceives its environment. This is, of course, also true for all other animals.

It may remain largely unknown how animals truly use their senses and what exactly they perceive with them. As always, humans can only compare the functionality of any kind of animal sense organs with their own and derive hypothetically what the animal does or might perceive with its own senses. Even more speculation and interpretation comes into play in attempts to describe the feelings that an animal might experience when it perceives scents, sounds, or images. Consider that various people subjectively perceive identical impressions differently. One person enjoys the scent of a rose, while someone else associates the same scent with sadness because of a painful experience, or simply considers it too sweet and heavy. It is incredibly more difficult, if not impossible, to understand exactly what animals sense.

The following descriptions of the sense organs of sharks do not claim to be complete. They only provide a foundation for later sections on shark-human interactions (see p. 113) and allow a glimpse of how sharks might use their senses when they encounter a person.

Hearing is the sense that, together with the nose, probably comes into play first when sharks perceive something over a great distance. Unlike humans, whose ears sit on the side of the head, the hearing organs of sharks are on the top of their heads. The two ear openings are so tiny that they can only be made out from a distance of 40-50 cm (15-20 in.) or closer. The shark's hearing organ, like that of humans, serves several functions. In addition to receiving sound waves, it is also able to recognize the position of the animal in the water, that is, its balance, and register acceleration during swimming. A big difference in human hearing seems to be that sharks can only hear low sounds at very low frequencies that probably do not exceed 600 Hz, that is, 600 oscillations per second. With their hearing, sharks can determine from which direction a sound originates. This is important for the animals, as their prey or other objects often only give away their position by producing sounds.

It is certain that the sense of hearing plays a large role in human-shark interaction. Every form of movement in water creates sound. Therefore it is always recommended to produce as little sound as possible when within sight of a shark, that is, to move as little as possible. During many experiments sharks reacted with particular sensitivity to knocking sounds.

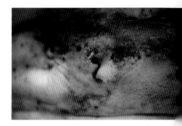

Nostrils of a seven-gill shark. Sharks have a good sense of smell and react selectively to different smells.

Smell and Taste

Much has been written about the shark's sense of smell. In popular science articles it is often compared to other animals. Such comparisons are useless because it does not matter how well a sense is developed in comparison to some other animal's. Every species of animal lives in its own unique environment and is subject to different requirements and challenges, in accordance with which its sense organs have developed differently along the evolutionary path: They simply are exactly as good as they need to be for them to survive in their natural habitat. Thus, sharks have exactly the olfactory sense organs that they need.

In general, two forms of perceiving scents can be distinguished in sharks. There are species of shark, such as the nurse shark, that are capable of determining the change in concentration of a substance in the water. They will swim in the direction of increasing concentration to reach the source of a scent, and can thus find their prey even if there is no current.

The other species of shark, for example tiger sharks, bull sharks, and others, require a current to find the source of a scent. After the scent is first perceived, they turn into the current and swim against it towards its source. Since the current is the primary guide, it can happen that the shark swims past the source of food and requires additional visual cues to precisely locate the prey.

The assumption that the characteristic constant left-and-right movement of the head serves to determine differences in scent concentration on the two nose holes is wrong. The head movements are simply a component of the swimming motion.

While the nose serves to recognize smells, the actual sense of taste is in taste buds on the roof of the mouth. These taste buds can be found primarily on the palate, but in small numbers also in other areas of the mouth. Whether sharks are capable of distinguishing the four basic tastes, "sweet," "sour," "salty," and "bitter" is not known. The taste buds, however, play a central role in shark accidents, since this sense is used by the shark to determine what kind of "object" a human might be. Using a so-called "exploratory bite," the shark obtains information about an unknown object or a person (see p. 92).

In this context the following is important: It can be considered certain that sharks are not motivated by the human scent in their interactions with humans. Smell only plays a role if a person dives or snorkels next to or in a current that also carries the scent of bait that has been laid out to catch fish.

The colors of dive suits do not seem to affect interaction with sharks.

Eyes

Next to the teeth, the eyes are a favorite topic in shark descriptions. However, the most frequently used terms "dead," "staring," or "bad eyesight" are far removed from the actual abilities of this sense. Shark eyes are highly developed and one can assume that they can see well and distinguish colors.

When the shark eye is compared anatomically with the human eye, they turn out to have much in common, such as a change in the pupil size when the light changes, rod and cone cells, and eye colors that vary by the individual. An essential difference, however, is in how focusing works: Sharks do not change the

Open and closed eye, accomplished by closing the nictitating membrane. This skin is sometimes called the third eyelid. Sharks can probably move it up reflexively as well as "voluntarily."

Eye of a seven-gill shark. The eyes are anatomically similar to those of humans. The biggest difference is that the lense is not deformed but moved back and forth to adjust focus.

shape of the lens but move it back and forth. Another difference is a mechanism of the shark eye that acts as an amplifier for small amounts of light and allows the animals to direct twice as much light as there is actually present onto the retina during low light conditions.

Great white sharks often raise their heads out of the water and seem to be looking around—similar to orcas. Are they perhaps scanning the surface for prey because the visibility underwater is often very poor? Hunted sea lions often perform characteristic jumps out of the water when fleeing. Is it therefore conceivable that sharks have developed this capability to clearly see prey when they pursue sea lions? That sharks generally stick their heads out of the water with their eyes open can also be observed in other species, such as blue or tiger sharks.

#1: Series of pictures in this book are extracted from video recordings, therefore…

#2: …of lesser quality. A great white shark is offered food. It…

This is why the question of how great white sharks can use their eyes outside the water is the topic of many detailed studies. Underwater, most sharks seem to be slightly far-sighted, but it is not clear how well they can focus in air.

It must be assumed that sharks are primarily visual animals when close up; that is, the eyes are their most important sense. This assumption is suggested by behaviors such as eye rolling (seeming and real) and head turning. If one is in proximity to a shark, one may notice that each eye seems to be wandering and moving back and forth. Typical and generally known are the sideways movements of the head and upper body of sharks during swimming. During these movements the eyes also move: The shark focuses on a certain point. When the head moves away by about 10°, that is farther ahead (in the swimming direction), the focus is eventually fixed on a new point. This creates a seeming forward and backward turning of the eye, which in reality is nothing but the continuing readjustment of the eye position in response to head movement.

#3:...ascends steeply from below. When great white sharks grab prey...

#4: ...they roll their eyes backwards into their head for protection, as shown in this series of images.

A great white shark is waiting for food at the surface.

A tiger shark at the surface: Tiger sharks are the only species in this family that do not have placental embryo development.

In addition, there is also actual rolling of the eyes, where the animal focuses on an object, for example, a human at the "inner circle" or in the "interzone" (see p. 129), and follows it with its eyes. When a shark encounters a person and pays attention to him or her, its eyes do not move in accordance with the head movements anymore, but remain focused on the person. The shark focuses on the person while swimming for as long as it is physiologically possible. The line/direction of sight is in this case moved significantly farther towards the front or back and kept in position unlike when swimming normally and not focusing on a particular object. In most cases this is only possible over a certain distance, because at some point the shark cannot turn its eyes farther towards the back and thus must turn its head in order to continue to focus on the object of interest. The "funnel of focus" is the total area covered by both eyes, that is, where the fields of vision of both eyes overlap. In most cases of shark-human interaction, the human is seen at the

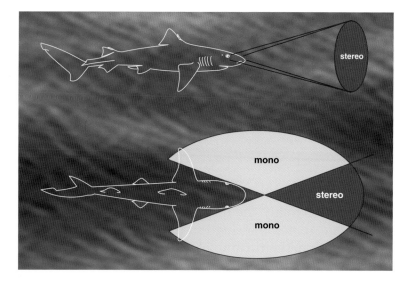

Schematic representation of the field of view of sharks.

fringes of this funnel of focus and not at its center. In order to put the human at the center of its funnel of focus and see it with both eyes, the shark would have to swim directly towards the human. This almost never happens. Usually, sharks approach humans from the side. Thus the animal sees them only with one eye.

This raises the question of whether an object even has to be near the center of the shark's field of vision, or whether it is sufficient for the animal, maybe even better, to observe an object at the periphery. The latter might have advantages: If the shark approaches something directly and frontally, it limits its escape paths, which in a first contact situation with something strange does not make sense. If an object is approached somewhat from the side and observed only with one eye, the path remains open in the direction in which the animal is swimming.

If an animal approaches sideways and then turns its head so that the object moves into the center of its field of vision, the situation requires a different interpretation (it is rare that a shark approaches sideways and then turns its whole body to focus on the object or

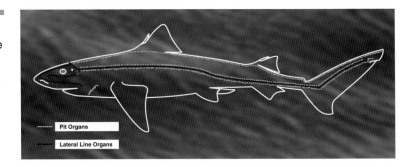

The pit and lateral line organs of sharks sense changes in water pressure.

Pit Organs

Lateral Line Organs

person by moving it into the center of its field of vision, usually only the head is turned). In this case the animal remains facing the direction in which it is swimming but the turning of the head reduces its hydrodynamic properties increasing drag. This behavior in turn suggests that the animal's curiosity has been awakened. Once the shark has turned its head, one can assume that it is interested in the situation and will express this. The shark will change direction and approach.

Mechanosensory Systems

Sharks have several sense organs with which they can sense water pressure. Since the research in these areas has not penetrated very far, how they work is mostly unclear. Sharks have both lateral line systems, such as are found in bony fishes (sharks are not fish), as well as pit organs. The latter are similar in construction to the cells of the lateral line system but are scattered over the whole back, as well as along the actual lateral lines, over the tail region, in between the pectoral fins, and even on the underside of the head. It may be said that these organs serve primarily to detect changes in water pressure. If a shark swims past an object at a distance of two to three body lengths, it can detect the water displacement caused by this object. It is unclear how these detected differences in pressure are processed. Do the sharks simply notice the water pressure as such, or can they perhaps create a kind of "pressure map" that provides them with information on the size and shape of the object? Perhaps sharks are even able to push water against the object and then process the "echo" similarly to sonar. From experiments it is known what the lateral lines and the pit organs measure, but how the shark actually uses these senses is at this time unknown.

In addition to these organs, there are also the spiracular organ and the vesicles of savi, which also fall into the category of mechanosensory organs. They can be found relatively closely together in the head area.

The first of those, the spiracular organ, seems to control the upper jaw. After an animal has bitten, the upper jaw, which is pushed towards the front during biting, must be aligned properly with the skull again. This realignment also requires proper positioning of muscles and ligaments. It must be assumed that this—should the upper jaw apparatus not have realigned

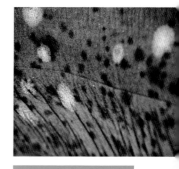

Lateral line of a seven-gill shark. The organ serves to sense changes in water pressure.

The barbels of nurse sharks are probably used to sense vibrations.

properly after a bite—triggers yawning, a behavior which is described later (p. 49).

The second organ is the vesicles of savi. They have also not been studied much. It is suspected, that these organs are able to sense vibrations in the ground.

Sensing Electricity and Heat

When sharks are relatively close to a living being, they can sense its electrical discharges. These discharges are also known as bioelectrical fields. Every time a muscle contracts, this kind of discharge occurs. Since bioelectrical fields are very weak, sharks must swim very close (probably only a few inches) to an object to sense it. This means that a shark must allow an object or approach an object far into its "inner circle" to use this ability.

The organs that perceive bioelectrical fields are the so-called ampoules of Lorenzini. They can be found in dense arrangements primarily in the area of the snout, and also less densely arranged in the mouth and around the eyes. These organs can be distinguished as small dark dots. They can sense voltage differences in the microvolt range.

Recent studies have also shown that the ampoules of Lorenzini cannot only sense electricity but also differences in temperature. This makes sense: Even though most marine organisms (except for marine mammals, some species of fish such as tuna, and some species of shark) have about the same body temperature as the surrounding water, they all produce heat as soon as their muscles contract when they move. This heat is not retained within the body, but emitted into the surrounding water. The sharks can most likely sense this heat.

It also seems likely that a shark that is close by will try to use its ampoules of Lorenzini to gather electrical and thermal information about the object, be it prey or a person.

The pointy teeth of the sand tiger shark are for grabbing fish and are less suitable for cutting up prey.

The hand is touching the shark near the mouth, which triggers snapping at the object. Most sharks react similarly when something touches the areas around the mouth.

It is not unusual that sharks will bump their snout into potential prey or other objects or touch them lightly with their body in passing; in the rare case of the object being a human, this is often interpreted as a shark incident. It seems clear that this kind of touch only serves to evaluate the object in question. Sharks have cells all over the body that will respond when the skin is stretched or pressure is applied to it.

Sensing Pressure and Skin Flexing

Great white shark investigates a decoy by touching it. In immediate proximity of an object, a shark is able not only to measure its bioelectrical field but also the heat that emanates from it.

Blind Spots

If one considers the large spectrum of sensory organs with which sharks are equipped, it seems almost impossible that there is a single area on their body with which they cannot perceive and analyze objects. Yet, there are obvious blind spots, which vary for each shark species. Especially in hammerhead sharks it is

#1: A bull shark is interacting...

#2: ... with a person during...

often observed that one hammerhead sharks approaches another from behind unnoticed and then whacks it with its "hammer" at the root of the tail. This leads to the conclusion that a hammerhead shark is not capable of recognizing what approaches from behind or above. The purpose of this hitting behavior needs to be studied. Since these whacks often cause clear dents, the behavior seems to be very intentional and goal oriented—perhaps playing a role in establishing a hierarchy.

Blind spots can also be observed in Caribbean reef sharks (*Carcharhinus perezi*) and blacktip sharks (*Carcharhinus limbatus*). If such an area exists on the upper side of the shark body, it is conceivable that there might also be one on the underside. This hypothesis is confirmed by my personal observations: Often, when I approached a shark from below and behind, the shark only noticed me if it turned its head far to the side, so that it was looking towards the back.

Sharks—or at least the bull sharks, great white sharks, and lemon sharks with which we work—all

#3: ... an experiment about stressful situations...

#4: ...between humans and sharks.

Even though sharks have very well-developed sense organs, they also have "blind regions" where they cannot register the presence of a person or other animal. Depending on species, these regions vary in size.

have a funnel shaped blind spot on their body. Its tape is near the second dorsal fin, and it widens towards the tail.

That the pit organs or the lateral lines do not seem to function in that region, could signify that these organs are oriented towards the side and front.

The question is whether these blind spots exist perhaps because previously existing sense organs have atrophied, or whether there never were any sense organs in this region, or only sense organs that "looked" forward. I suspect, that it was never necessary for sharks to be able to notice a being approaching from above or behind during their long evolutionary

history. Otherwise, the necessary sense organs would have evolved, or the pit organs and lateral lines would also work towards the rear.

Individual Space

Like any other animal, a shark cannot be approached without encountering boundaries (even in the blind spot this is not exactly easy). No animal permits this without reacting in one way or another. There is a boundary, which when crossed, will trigger flight or aggression towards the invader. This is also true for the shark. It is surrounded by an "inner circle" and an "outer circle" of individual space, and crossing into each of these spaces by a living being triggers a reaction. If a human violates the outer circle—either by swimming towards the shark or because the shark approaches him or her—the shark will usually display a first reaction to the position of the human. If the human enters the inner circle of the shark, which extends around the shark to a distance of about two times the length of its body, he or she has entered the individual space (see details p. 129), and the shark will react unambiguously.

It is important to understand the individual spaces of a shark in order to be able to interpret its behaviors. Most interactions and observations take place when humans are in between the outer and inner circles, that is, the "interzone." In this zone a human can observe the shark, and there is no risk of the shark being cornered, unable to escape, or limited in its withdrawal options. If the shark is more interested in the person, it will approach closer until the person gets into the individual space, that is, the inner circle, of the animal. Being closer obviously gives the shark further opportunity for studying the object. Now that

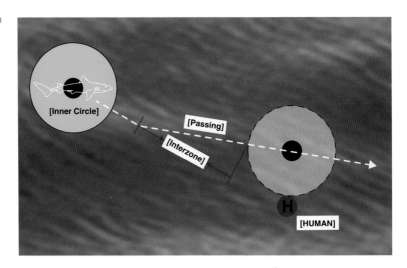

A shark approaches a human (H). The dotted line indicates the swim direction of the animal. The space between where the shark first reacts in reference to the human's position and the shark's individual space ("inner circle") is called "interzone."

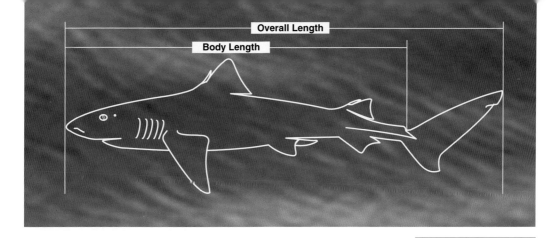

Overall Length

Body Length

the object or human is close, the shark can correctly analyze water displacement with its lateral line system. Since water particles are only disturbed slightly by movement because of the inertia of water, sharks can recognize such movement only when they are very close to the object. It is possible that the reach of this sense correlates to the size of the individual space of sharks.

As a rule of thumb it can be said that such changes in pressure can be perceived at a distance of about twice the body length of the shark, and this distance is also in most cases equivalent to the radius of the inner circle.

Important: When working with sharks using distances, one should never use absolute values in meters or feet, only body lengths. Absolute distances do not say anything about the intentions of an animal, relative distances—in relationship to the body length of the animal—however, do. For example, suppose that two animals swim about 5 m (15 ft.) away from a person, one of them is 2 m (6.5 ft.) long, the other one at 1 m (3.2 ft.) only half that size. It can be assumed that the larger animal, which is only 2 1/2 times its body length away from the object, is more likely to have intentions in regard to that object than the smaller animal, which is five body lengths away.

The length of a shark can be given in two ways, either as body length or as overall length including the tail.

If the shark remains at a constant distance to an object, it begins to circle it. This circling was previously—and is sometimes still today—equated with a

Continuous Circling

When a suckerfish attaches to a shark, sense organs are often irritated. The shark may react by trying to shake off the suckerfish.

shark attack. As is often the case in daily life with other people, in the context of sharks it is easy to assign a negative context to something before taking the time to reflect on an unexplainable circumstance and look for the true cause.

Circling in sharks has not been studied much. In my opinion, continuous circling is only another version of using the concept of individual distance. It seems obvious that it means that the animal is interested in an object. It is unclear however, why sharks continue to circle over longer periods of time. It is conceivable that they would like to "palpitate" the objects with their various senses over a longer period. It is also

Great white sharks circle around a decoy in order to examine the object.

possible that circling is simply a kind of displacement activity that arises from the conflict between an impulse to swim away or approach. Because neither desire wins out, circling results. Sharks fundamentally never attack something or somebody that is unfamiliar—they first try to find out who and what the unknown object is. Whatever the motivator or trigger for continuous circling, sharks that do it must be given the greatest attention, because it is always possible that a shark may cross the inhibition threshold to approach and actually approach.

Swim Patterns

When a shark approaches a human it can swim above, below, or at the same level. In addition, the shark can approach directly from the front or at an angle from the side, which is always less than 90°. From this basic pattern derive specific primary swim patterns that are followed during interactions. The first four swim patterns listed below (passing by, frontal and lateral approach, and circling around) are usually executed at the same level.

Especially for scuba divers it is helpful (in particular for underwater photographers) to be able to recognize and distinguish between the different swim patterns. Depending on the swim pattern one can assume that the animal is more or less goal oriented in its actions. Passing by is the most commonly seen swim pattern. Especially on a reef, a shark that just passes by will rarely turn around and come back. The other behaviors are more oriented towards the object and indicate that the animal has an interest in it (note that passing by acquires a different meaning when it happens in open water). A human only has to be concerned about ascending great white sharks. Because ascending from below is one of the typical attack strategies of a great white shark.

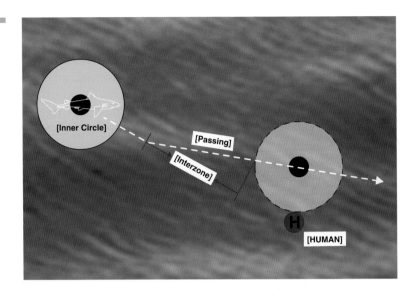

When sharks make a pass, their individual space ("inner circle") touches the personal space of the human.

[Inner Circle]

[Passing]

[Interzone]

H

[HUMAN]

Passing by

The first swim pattern is "passing by." As the name suggests, the animal swims past a person and does not approach closer than the individual distance. The human does not at all or barely touch the outside of the shark's inner circle (see p. 129). Often, passing by is the first in a series of swim patterns, if the animal develops further interest in an object.

Frontal Approach

The second often observed swim pattern is the frontal approach (see explanatory figure on p. 41, top). It first resembles passing by, but the animal swims more directly towards the person, then turns away before crossing the threshold of the inner circle and swims off more or less in the direction from which it came—the shark does more or less a 180° U turn. Such a swim pattern suggests a very great interest of the animals in the person. It is possible that the shark is trying to find out by means of a more direct approach, whether the object will take flight like potential prey or will generally show prey-like reactions.

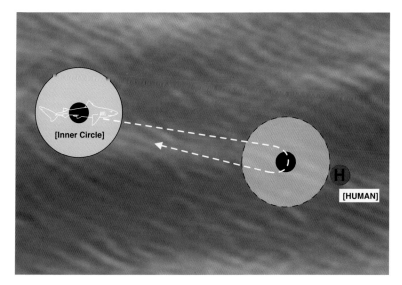

[Inner Circle]

[HUMAN]

When approaching frontally, the shark swims directly towards a person, turns away shortly before reaching him or her, and swims away in the direction from which it came. How closely the shark approaches depends on the size of its "inner circle."

In addition to the frontal there is also a lateral approach swim pattern (see figure on p. 42, top). As the name indicates, the shark approaches a person from the side. It does not swim directly towards the person but slightly offset. In immediate proximity of the person, usually arrived at after passing by, the shark

Lateral Approach

In shallow water, bull sharks often swim in pairs. Their reason for this "pairing up" has not been studied yet.

When approaching from the side, the animal passes over the person, turns around, and then makes a second pass. On the second pass, the lateral line organs seem to be involved.

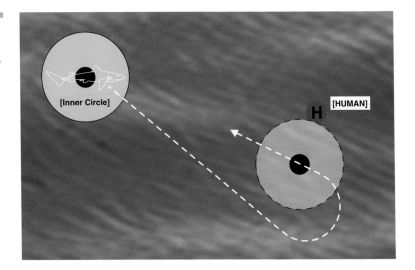

turns towards the person and then returns to its initial position. On the second pass, the animal approaches closer, close enough to be able to use its lateral line system, which is not possible during the first pattern, the actual passing by, or the frontal approach. With this swim pattern, the inner circle of the shark touches the human, and the shark usually approaches to a distance of two body lengths.

"Circling around once" is comparable to "circling," where the shark chooses a distance from the object that equals the radius of its "inner circle."

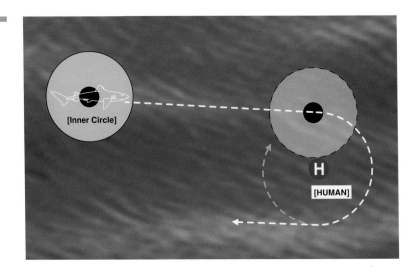

The fourth swimming approach pattern consists of circling the person, where the shark approaches to the inner circle. It swims around the person at a distance of about two body lengths and is able to use its lateral line system. Usually, the animal will continue to swim away in the direction from where it has come after a certain amount of time. In rare cases, this swim pattern can develop into "continuous circling."

The fifth swim pattern is rarely observed and primarily found in great white sharks: it is the "vertical ascent." The shark approaches from relatively directly below and only turns away when the boundary of the individual space of the object is reached. This swim pattern is a typical attack strategy of the great white shark. It does not necessarily mean that the person is considered prey. But this choice of approach must be watched with full attention.

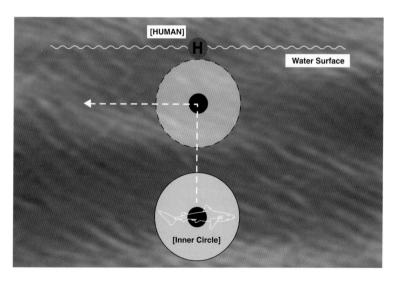

Ascending is often seen in great white sharks. The animal ascends vertically towards the person and turns away when it reaches a distance equal to the radius of its "inner circle."

There is an additional swim pattern, called "patrolling." The animal only approaches close enough to be able to visually perceive the object (largest possible distance where eye contact is still possible) and executes a variety of swim patterns there. Unlike all the other described situations, the shark shows a certain interest in the situation but does not approach.

Patrolling consists of a combination of different swimming patterns executed at the periphery of the visual field. The animal does not approach.

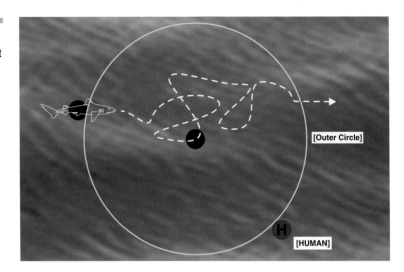

[Outer Circle]

H [HUMAN]

Swimming Speed

Recognizing swimming speeds is part of analyzing body language. Together with the chosen angle of approach (see p. 126) they are good indicators of the intentions of the animal.

In order to properly assess a shark, it is also necessary to consider its swimming speed—in this case of course the purpose is less to measure the absolute speed of the animal in question, but rather to compare and assess it in relationship to other experiences of encountering sharks. A speedometer is not necessary for this, because this assessment is not done in miles per hour.

In order to estimate the speed of a shark, the frequency at which the tail moves is used as an indicator. The observer focuses on tail movements and counts them. After a few seconds, a sense for the rhythm sets in. If this remembered rhythm is later used for comparison, one can quickly assess whether the speed of the shark has changed or not. In most cases, sharks swim a little faster (increased beat) near the inner circle boundary and in the interzone, or as far away as the boundary of the outer circle.

When working with large sharks, the position of the animal when it changes speed in relationship to its individual spaces is significant. It gives important information on a possible change in intention of the animal for the given situation.

For example, if a shark is about two body lengths away from a person (it is therefore near its inner circle) and it suddenly accelerates, one must assume that the shark feels threatened; on the other hand, if one sees it accelerate in the interzone, one can assume that this shark is cautious. I have almost never (!) seen an animal accelerate in the interzone in order to directly swim towards me. I only observed this behavior a few times and only when I intentionally attracted the animal with bait. The shark probably increased its speed because other sharks, potentially competing for the food, were nearby.

Bull sharks often swim in very shallow water. This can lead to stress reactions since in shallow water, escape routes are very limited.

A bull shark is checking me out.

Active and Passive Approaches

All previously mentioned swimming approach patterns are considered passive approaches, where "passive" refers to the more or less motionless behavior of the person being approached. If a person or an object does not move, the shark can focus on something stationary and therefore does not need to constantly change and adapt its swim patterns.

In an "active" approach the object or person also changes position, so that the animal constantly has to adjust its movement pattern. If one wishes to interact with a shark, one should first offer the opportunity for a passive approach—this is done simply by remaining motionless. One gives oneself the opportunity to observe the behavior of the animal. Once one is familiarized with the situation and the animal, one can begin to trigger reactions and swim patterns in the animal by moving.

I do not mean by this that a shark should be cornered or provoked. One can simply actively (!) close the distance to the animal slightly, for example, by swimming towards it, and observe what happens. If the shark is interested in the situation, it will usually—like any shy animal—retreat a little, but it will not swim away, but will try to reestablish the original distance, and thus control the situation by controlling the distance. This can be the beginning of an interaction with the shark.

Shark Behavior 101

If after the first phase of approach one has gained a first impression of the shark and the animal is in the interzone (see p. 129), it is now time to study the attitude (shortened to "A" in the interaction model) of the animal (see p. 135). "Attitude" is a very important part of my interaction model ADORE-SANE (Attitude, Direction, Origin, Relation, Environment-Situation, Activity, Nervousness, Experience), which I will introduce starting on page 122.

One problem when analyzing the attitude, that is, behavior patterns of sharks, is in the discomfort that often sets in when sharks show up, which prevents or gets in the way of a precise observation of the animal. This is why usually no details of an encounter are remembered; what is remembered is mostly expressed in generalized phrases, such as "the shark approached following the reef," "the shark was resting on the bottom," or "the shark was swimming in the distance." Never is it said that a shark is doing this or that

The half-open mouth is not related to threatening but simply a snapshot during "yawning."

because of at least an assumed reason. This is exactly one of the major reasons why we understand so little about sharks.

As mentioned in the first chapter of this book, not enough quiet time is made available to actually observe sharks and therefore the triggers of a course of action are usually not considered. Sharks do not swim aimlessly through the water, but like other animals, they are continuously affected by their environment (abbreviated as "E" in the interaction model) and led and driven by inherent impulses.

#1: "Yawning": The lower jaw, as if biting in slow motion, is…

#2: … pushed forward, in order to realign its position…

In order to better understand the behavior of sharks towards other sharks, other animals, and humans, it is urgently necessary to analyze the various behavior patterns and interpret them in a framework of the animal.

Generally, two different types of behavior patterns can be distinguished: internally triggered (without external influence and initiated by the animal itself) and externally triggered (initiated in response to external factors, such as sounds, scents, other sharks, or people).

Below, we shall describe some internally and externally triggered behaviors that can often be recognized by divers and snorklers, so that they can better understand the attitude (Att) of these animals.

Yawning and Gaping

Yawning and gaping are two movements of the mouth that are not related to feeding (see p. 77 for information on feeding behaviors). Unlike a bite, which rarely lasts more than half a second, the so-called yawning can often last three to four times as long. The process

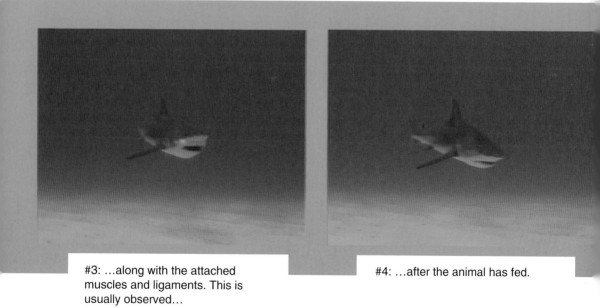

#3: ...along with the attached muscles and ligaments. This is usually observed...

#4: ...after the animal has fed.

A Caribbean reef shark is pursued by other members of its species because it is swimming off with a piece of food. Food creates competition, and sharks try to take away pieces of food that have not been swallowed by other sharks.

of yawning serves to reposition the jaws. In shark jaws, muscles, ligaments, and tendons are connected to the skull in a very complicated arrangement, and it can happen that these structures will not realign properly after biting. So, the jaws must be opened and closed one more time to arrange things properly. This process of yawning happens very slowly (with the exception of the actual moving forward of the upper jaw, which can only be done quickly since sharks have no muscles that could restrict this movement) and does guarantee that the various mouth parts will be aligned properly. In most cases, yawning once is sufficient. In rare cases it is necessary to repeat the process if the first time was not successful. Yawning is often combined with a sideways movement of the head.

In addition to this easily interpreted behavior, one can often see a shark open its mouth partially, where the upper jaw is never (!) moved forward and thus the teeth in the upper jaw do not become visible. This behavior is called gaping. Unlike yawning, which is only variable in its duration, gaping shows a large variety in the degree to which the mouth is opened and in duration. Gaping is a threatening gesture that is directed towards members of the same and other shark species, but also towards boats or humans, if the

Yawning Caribbean reef shark: Yawning is falsely interpreted as a threat. But when threatening the mouth is usually kept in a half-open position.

shark feels threatened. Gaping is usually sufficient to get a perceived opponent to retreat. If this is not the case, which especially may happen if there is a larger distance between the shark and its opponent, gaping is often combined with hunching.

Hunching

As the name indicates, the animal arches its back in this pattern of behavior. But this behavior does not just draw attention because of the obvious arching of the back, but also because of the resulting changed way of swimming, which is inhibited by the arched back. Like gaping, hunching can happen very quickly within fractions of a second. In this case, a change in the way the shark swims is not recognizable for humans—but it is for other sharks. If hunching continues for several seconds, it also becomes obvious to us.

What could this behavior mean? If one accepts the current literature, this behavior is the typical threatening behavior of sharks and is also called agonistic behavior. It assumes that the animals show such a grotesque behavior when they feel threatened by scuba divers, and that if the diver does not react, an attack is likely. But as convincing as this reasoning seems—and thus it has rarely been questioned in 30 years—a closer look reveals several open questions.

A suckerfish is detaching from a bull shark. This happens when this bony fish wants to move to a different location on the shark, when it has been dislodged by the shark's wiggling, when it is looking for a new host, or when it sees free-floating food. In this case, closeness to the water surface may also play a role.

A shark that arches its back does not swim in such a grotesque manner by choice, but because it is required to do so and cannot do differently with its back arched. The actual arching of the back seems to be a result of a raised snout combined with a pressing down of the dorsal fins. If this so-called threatening behavior is reduced to what the animal is actually doing actively, then it only changes the position of its snout and dorsal fins. If one observes a normally swimming shark from the side, the dorsal fins stick out to the side relatively horizontally. When the shark arches its

#1: A blacktip shark is trying to force a suckerfish…

#2: …that is attached on its lateral line to move. The shark is wiggling…

back, they are pressed down and lift up the sides of the body. This results in increased resistance to moving the body.

Changing the position of the dorsal fins can also be observed when a shark gets into a situation that requires a quick reaction. The changed position of the dorsal fins makes it possible for the shark to move quickly to one or the other side. Therefore, this part of the behavior should more likely be seen as a preventive measure than a threatening gesture. But what could the lifting of the snout indicate? Maybe a shark indicates in that way that it has recognized a threat, and as its response, it briefly abandons its streamlined shape? This may be conceivable, since every animal with a distinctly hydrodynamic body shape would recognize this—provided it knows about the natural body shape of the other animal. This is the case for members of the same species, but not usually for a diver who misinterprets the behavior of the shark.

Independent of this, there is an important problem in that hunching has only been observed thoroughly in

#3: ...so that the affected area of its skin is contracted or stretched...

#4: ...in order to dislodge the sucker (a modified dorsal fin) of the fish.

one species of shark, the gray reef shark (Carcharhinus amblyrhynchos), but not in any of the other closely related sharks. Why only in this species? Could it be that only one species has evolved such a behavior and just for encounters with humans, but not any of the other closely related species? Certainly not! The lack of such a threatening behavior in the other species, which also come into contact with people, puts doubts on the current interpretation of this behavior.

Because the target group—that is humans—was not part of the evolutionary development of sharks during millions of years (and humans definitely were not!), the development of such a targeted behavior is not just improbable, but simply impossible. Therefore one must consider that this so-called threatening behavior probably does not exist in reality, but that hunching has simply been misinterpreted. In my opinion, sharks did not develop this behavior for humans, but generally to handle conflict or uncomfortable situations, primarily between members of the same or other species of sharks. An additional option will be described in detail below.

A swim pattern that looks exactly (!) like hunching is called pseudo-agonistic behavior, or wiggling, or MAAD (Mistakenly Assumed Agonistic Display). It is triggered by suckerfish that attach to sharks or slide along their body. A suckerfish is a bony fish whose first dorsal fin has been modified to form a sucker, so that it can attach to sharks, rays, sea turtles, or other large fish. MAAD's exclusive purpose may be to stretch or wrinkle an irritated skin area to reduce the amount of suction from the fish. This forces the suckerfish to reattach or find a different spot on the body, which is what happens in most cases.

Where the suckerfish is attached this can cause pronounced movement patterns, which can also look like the hunching described on page 51—for example, if suckerfish attach around or near the sense organs of

Blacktip reef shark at the "inner circle." They will rarely cross this threshold.

the shark. A sense organ that reacts very sensitively is the lateral line system. If a suckerfish attaches to it, this might trigger false sensory input (disturbances) and make it more difficult or even impossible for the shark to recognize changes in water pressure. Equally, near the ears or in the snout area suckerfish can trigger corresponding reactions.

Similar behaviors can also be seen in body areas that are hydrodynamically sensitive. The base of the pectoral fins must be mentioned in particular. Studies of the function of shark pectoral fins suggest that these fins are similar to the wings of an airplane in regards to lift and flow. It can thus be suspected that a suckerfish at the base of a pectoral fin changes the flow of water, or even interrupts it, so that the shark could get into the equivalent of a tailspin, to which it must react.

Suckerfish have been around for millions of years and the behavior patterns of their hosts are very pronounced. Interestingly, these patterns can change from species to species, and some species react more intensely than others to irritation of the same area.

Gill Splaying

Sharks do not actively move their gills when they swim, but the water runs over them passively as they move. After a shark has fed, it can happen that pieces of food get stuck in the gills so that they must be cleaned. To this end, an increased amount of water is pumped through the gills, which causes them to splay. In order to accomplish this, the lower jaw is pressed against the palate and the gills are actively closed at the same time. Then, in repid succession the lower jaw is pushed down and fractions of seconds later the gills are reopened. This quick opening of the mouth reduces pressure, which results in a current when the gills are opened. If food leftovers are in the gill area, they are usually dislodged by this current. Even though this behavior is usually performed intentionally, it can also be triggered by suckerfish or parasites that attach to the gills and irritate the shark.

Twitching

Twitching or shivering is familiar in cows or horses that are being bothered by flies. The skin in the affected areas contracts repeatedly and very rapidly.

#1: Blacktip shark is trying to scrape off a sucker fish…

#2: …that has attached to its side. If suckerfish…

Splaying of gills: This can happen when either bits of food leftovers remain in the gills, parasites have taken a foothold, or suckerfish attached themselves.

Something similar can be observed in sharks when they are irritated by suckerfish. Not all skin regions seem to be able to twitch—and often the fins will also tremble, especially the pectoral fins.

#3: …attach near important sense organs, the sense organs are irritated….

#4: …and give the shark false information.

A blacktip shark is "rolling" on the bottom to get rid of a suckerfish attached to its side.

Chaffing

If a shark is so irritated by a suckerfish that it really wants to get rid of it, it will rub the affected spot on the ground and try to chafe off the fish. If this does not succeed, it will try jumping out of the water. The shark accelerates towards the surface, jumps, and splashes back onto the water surface with the side of the body to which the suckerfish is attached.

Clasper Splaying

Independent of the reproductive period, it can be observed in some species of shark, that the males will splay one of their claspers (external male sexual organs). The reason for this is unknown. However if a suckerfish is attached, it seems to be the trigger.

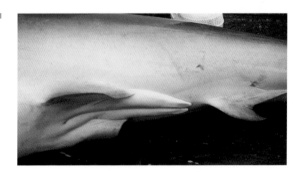

Male sexual organ (clasper): Even though claspers come in pairs, only one of them is functional for mating.

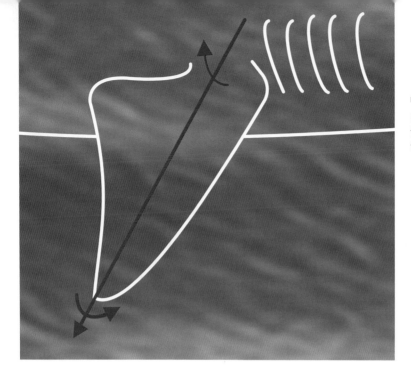

Dorsal fins are very flexible and can be turned in all directions.

Fin Language

Whenever there are objects in the interzone or even the inner circle of a shark, movements of the pectoral fins become clearly distinguishable. The pectoral fins direct most movements of the shark. Even though one can not really speak of gestures, the pectoral fins indicate often quite clearly what the intentions of the animal are. It is a fact that a shark's intention is also expressed in the angle at which it approaches, and this angle is quickly adjusted by using the pectoral fins—especially when actively approaching (a human).

If the pectoral fins of sharks are studied, it can be seen that they are always slightly turned upwards along their longitudinal axis. (Note: The basic position of the pectoral fins is not horizontally away from the body, but turned up slightly.) This is because these fins counteract tail movement. With its every move the tail effects a slight downward movement, which is counteracted by the pectoral fins. Since sharks do not just swim horizontally, but also up and down, it can easily be deduced that their pectoral fins must have a large range of motion.

The pectoral fins of sharks are a good starting point for learning about the basic body language of these animals. They play a role in many behaviors. Below, four of these behaviors, which are directly related to the position of the pectoral fins, are described. The first three have to do with swim patterns; the fourth is a cleaning behavior.

Turning Down

Whenever an object approaches the inner circle of a shark or the shark actively brings an object in there, one of the pectoral fins is turned downwards—always the one that makes it possible to turn away from the object (!). The longitudinal axis of the fin can assume an almost vertical position. The other pectoral fin remains horizontal. This one-sided pressing down and slightly turning forward of the underside creates an increase in water resistance, which cause the rest of the body to rotate around this fin. From a greater distance, the positions of the pectoral fins are difficult to determine because it often takes only small changes to turn the body.

Maneuvering

Sometimes a shark presses down not one but both pectoral fins; for example, when a human approaches its inner circle. This behavior is often interpreted as aggression. However, the shark only puts itself into a position where it can react faster. Pressing down the pectoral fins increases—as mentioned earlier—the ability of the shark to maneuver. By pressing down the pectoral fins, the lateral body surface is increased, so that the shark can quickly turn away towards either side. It is understandable that this pressing down of

the fins is often misinterpreted as aggressive behavior, because on one hand it looks quite unnatural—normally the pectoral fins of a shark stick out horizontally—and on the other hand, when the pectoral fins are pressed down, the shark swims jerkily. Since the head remains quite still, this way of swimming really looks very threatening—and is often misinterpreted.

Another reason for the assumption of seeming aggressive behavior may also have to do with the biased experiences of the observers. Many divers have experience with sharks, in most cases reef sharks. In some diving areas one sees mostly the same species and eventually acquires a certain amount of experience with its members. One would know how such an

Bull sharks usually swim close to the bottom and are hard to see.

animal would normally approach, at what angle it would approach, which speed it would choose, and so on. One acquires a certain "feel" for the species. If someone frequently dives with a species whose representatives usually turn away at a distance of 4–5 m (12.8–16 ft.) (radius of their inner circle), sooner or later this distance becomes a point of reference. And this can then lead to the assumption of apparent aggression in another species: If someone now dives at a different location, where the animals that live there have a smaller threshold (inner circle), they will of course approach closer and cross the threshold established in the memory of the diver. Such a crossing of perceived boundaries triggers feelings of discomfort or even panic—which then results in a report stating that the shark "clearly acted aggressively." But the animals of unfamiliar species show equally little aggression as those with whom one is already "up close and personal."

Braking

Sharks cannot brake well actively, because, for one, they cannot reverse their swimming motions like many species of fish can. However, they are capable of stopping quickly. This only works if they also change direction at the same time; otherwise, they can brake, but their momentum (inertia) may still cause them to collide with the object. In order to stop completely, sharks press both pectoral fins down, turn them in a right angle to their direction of swimming, lift their head, and angle the front of their body to turn to the side. Such braking maneuvers can frequently be observed when sharks are surprised. Such a surprise situation can arise, when one suddenly turns towards a shark that is approaching from behind, or enters the inner sphere of a shark that is swimming above or at the same level. The shark has to react quickly, and it can happen that the shark almost collides with the person.

A rarer but more surprising behavior is the so-called "wipe off." It also counts among the behavior patterns triggered by suckerfish. It frequently happens that a suckerfish attaches directly behind a pectoral fin (for example near the lateral line), which irritates the shark. In such cases I have observed that the shark turned the affected pectoral fin down, so that it was able to use it to swipe the sucker fish off the body, as with a shovel.

Wipe-off

Behavior and Interest

- The animal has no interest in the person   ++ The animal has increased interest
+ The animal has some interest   +++ The animal has great interest

Behavior/Movement	Interest/ Influence
Swimming directly towards a person	+++
Small angle when approaching	++
Large angle when approaching	+/−
Passing	+/−
Frontal approach	+++
Approach from the side	+++
Circling around once	+++
Ascending	+++
Patrolling	+
Circling continuously	+++
Increasing speed	+++
Swimming above the person (*)	−
Swimming at the same level as person (*)	+/−
Swimming below person (*)	+
Gaping	+++
Pressing down pectoral fins (**)	+++
MAAD	−
Chaffing	−
Eye rolling	+/−
Head turning (>inner circle)	++
Head turning (inner circle)	+++

*) Only limited interpretation without consideration of other criteria
**) The person must be close to the "inner circle."

Pages 64/65: A great white shark tries to bite a photographer's shadow on the water surface.

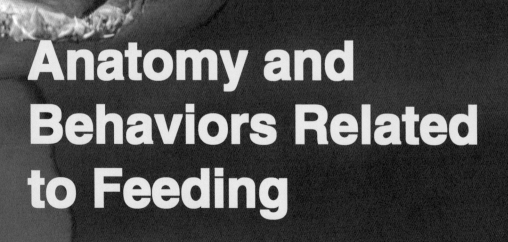

Anatomy and
Behaviors Related
to Feeding

Jaw bones of the largest great white shark ever caught in South Africa.

Sharks and Their Jaws

Most known shark swim patterns serve to obtain more information about an object, for example, a human. This works only up to a certain point, until the capacities of the various sense organs, such as lateral lines or ampoules of Lorenzini, are reached. In order to get conclusive information about an unknown object or human, the animal eventually has to bite using the so-called exploratory bite (see p. 92).

Sharks sometimes feature impressively large teeth. We humans rarely look at these teeth as normal tools for acquiring food—which is what they are—but from the point of view of how they can injure a person. Generally, the different teeth of different species of shark allow us to draw conclusions about their diet, as with other animals. In adaptation to their diet, some species developed slim and long teeth, wide serrated teeth, or flattened plate-like teeth.

In this chapter the jaws of sharks, their feeding behaviors, and their feeding strategies are discussed, which are in modified form sometimes also used when interacting with humans.

Jaws

Sharks have a limited number of teeth, which only varies slightly or not at all within a species and is species typical. Depending on the species, one can usually count no more than 10 to 20 teeth that are in active use in each half of the jaw. As for other types of animals, the number of teeth is expressed using a dental formula.

Unlike in mammals, shark teeth are not firmly anchored into the jaw cartilage, but sit loosely in a layer of connective tissue almost directly on top of the jaw bones. Therefore, they can easily be dislodged.

It was calculated that, for example, tiger sharks (*Galeocerdo cuvier*) produce 30,000-40,000 teeth over their lifetime. Depending on the species, a tooth is replaced after two to four weeks. The replacement frequency depends on the animal's level of activity (feeding) and the season. The colder the water, the slower the metabolism is.

Teeth in a row of teeth are not connected to each other. Each tooth is part of a kind of "conveyer belt," where several teeth at different stages of development are arranged in rows from back to front and pushed forward onto the jaw, so that every time a broken or worn tooth falls out, a new tooth becomes available. This is why it is sometimes called a "revolver jaw," because the teeth are "loaded" successively. Depending on the species of shark, five and more rows of fully formed teeth that are ready to serve as replacements can be counted.

Tiger sharks are the only large shark species that has the same types of teeth in the upper and lower jaws. This type of tooth is considered the most highly developed in sharks. The animal is able to cut and saw simultaneously when turning its head.

The teeth of a great white shark change over its lifetime from smaller and pointier to the well-known triangular serrated shape.

Jaw Protrusion

Not only the teeth, but also the mechanics of shark jaws are unique and have been the subject of many discussions. Especially in great white sharks the typical pushing forward of the upper jaw has often been shown in movies. The upper jaw is pushed down at high speed—which looks almost like a steam piston. This happens seemingly without effort. It also creates the impression that the upper jaw is not connected to the skull. This is not completely wrong, because the upper jaw and skull of a shark are only connected to each other with ligaments and muscles. Not only great white sharks are capable of freely moving their upper jaw, but also other large shark species, such as bull sharks, tiger sharks, and reef sharks.

The mouth of most sharks is positioned behind the tip of the snout, which is also called hyostyly. When a shark protrudes its upper jaw, the snout is pulled back and up at the same time, so that the jaw is not underneath it any more, but in the front of it. This makes it possible for sharks—independent of their position when they bite—to eat without rotating their body. All sharks create negative pressure inside their mouth before they bite, which creates suction. Only because of this suction effect can sharks grasp and bite their prey. The water in front of the snout would otherwise be pushed foward as the shark moved (because water cannot be compressed), and if the shark tried to bite, the water would be pushed away together with the prey. The suction created by the negative pressure inside the shark's mouth counteracts this effect.

Teeth Mirror the Diet

Each shark eats in a specific way. In order to optimally grab and hold on to prey, appropriate teeth are required. In the lower jaw, these teeth are usually narrow and pointed like daggers, in the upper jaw wider and serrated. The teeth in the lower jaw are primarily

Teeth of a seven-gill shark: unlike most other sharks, the teeth of the lower jaw are used for cutting up prey.

used to grasp and hold prey, while the teeth of the upper jaw are used to bite off pieces of meat. Serrated teeth cut (saw) in connection with the typical sideways

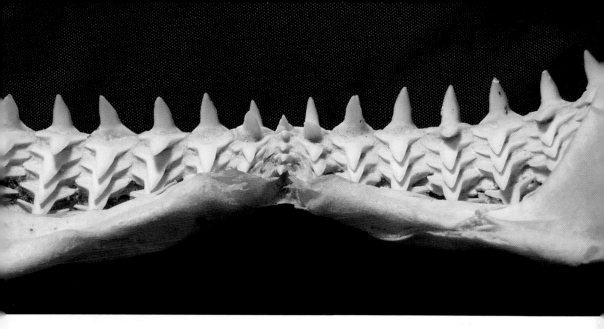

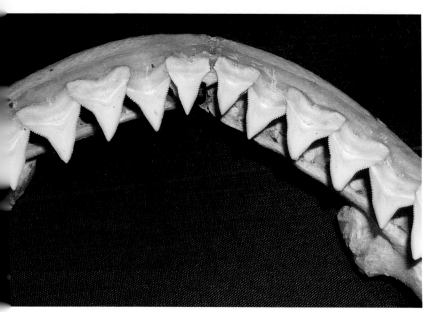

Teeth arranged in rows in the lower jaw of a shark. The teeth are only kept in place by connective tissue and can easily fall out. This type of arrangement is also called "revolver jaw."

Serrated and triangular teeth in the upper jaw of a bull shark: It can only cut up prey when the teeth are used like a saw.

movement of the head seen in feeding sharks. The lower jaw remains relatively immobile and holds on to the prey item. This way of eating is optimized, because the upper and lower jaws are not firmly connected to each other, but only attached by ligaments. Depending on the species of shark and the species-specific diet, prey may be swallowed whole and the teeth then serve

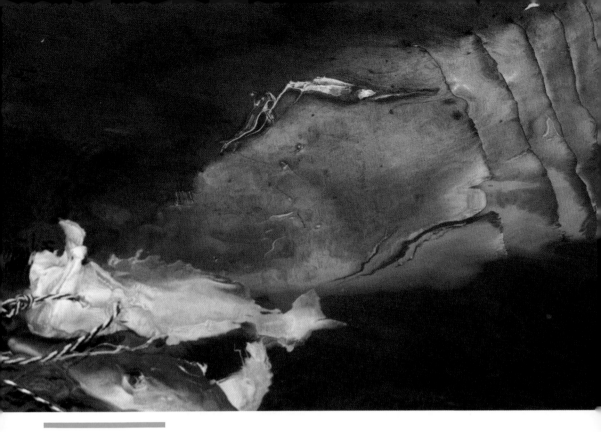

Bite injury on a great white shark by a member of its own species.

only to hold on to it. In this case, the teeth of the upper jaw are not serrated, because this would not be of any advantage, but are also dagger-like, like those of the lower jaw. However, even sharks that do not have clearly developed serrated teeth in the upper jaw can tear apart prey with raw strength and appropriate jerking of the head. In general, it can be said that sharks have highly developed teeth that are constructed exactly like human teeth. Shark teeth also have tooth enamel, a cavity, blood vessels, and nerves. The largest difference to human dentition is in tooth development and the "revolver jaw."

Teeth of the Tiger Shark

The tiger shark has the most versatile teeth of all sharks. This species is often considered primitive because its reproduction is less highly developed than that of other representatives of the same family. The highly developed teeth, however, lead to a contrary conclusion. The teeth of tiger sharks have both a sawing and a cutting surface, so that the prey is caught and cut up at the same time while the head is moved back and forth. This is an advantage over how other sharks cut up their prey and makes the tiger shark considerably more efficient than other sharks whose teeth do not have cutting surfaces. It is therefore not surprising that the teeth in the upper and lower jaws of tiger sharks are the same. Because of their teeth tiger sharks can choose from a large variety of prey,

Since more muscles are attached to the lower jaw, it is usually more massive than the upper jaw.

so that they depend less on availability and are less affected by fluctuation in availability of single types of prey. One could say that the tiger shark has specialized to be an all-animal-eater. Its diet includes birds and fish, but also turtles and other sharks. That one has found items like license plates, nails, or other things in the stomachs of tiger sharks should not be given too much significance: it is not known what the animal actually ate when it took in those items, since the soft parts had already been digested by the time the shark was caught.

Feeding Strategies

Feeding strategies, just like swim patterns, can differ between species. For example, a nurse shark, which prefers to feed on bottom dwelling animals, swims differently from a great white shark that hunts seals at the surface. It is important to remember a shark

Feeding Strategies and Hunting Behaviors of Selected Shark Species

"Gouger" refers to a species whose members feed on large prey and are only able to tear off pieces; they cannot swallow their prey whole like the "swallowers."

Species	Feeding Strategy	Diet of Adults
Blue shark (*Prionace glauca*)	Usually sucks in whole prey item. Can also bite into larger (dead) prey and bite off chunks using sawing motions.	Primarily a "swallower," sometimes a "gouger." Diet: Squid, cephalopods, small fish, occasionally small sharks, whale carcasses, or birds, can also feed on plankton.
Bull shark (*Carcharhinus leucas*)	Direct biting usually in connection with slight rolling, but may also just lift the snout without rolling, and then bite. This shark is known for grasping large prey and "sawing off" pieces. Usually attacks slowly.	"Gouger" and "swallower." Diet: Fish (various species), sharks (mostly young of hammerhead sharks, reef sharks, bull sharks, etc.), rays, skates, dolphins, whales, turtles; occasionally crabs and other invertebrates.
Gray reef shark (*Carcharhinus amblyrhynchos*)	Feeds near the bottom.	Primarily a "swallower." Diet: Mostly small fish, cephalopods, lobster.
Great hammerhead shark (*Sphyrna mokarran*)	Often uses its "hammer" to beat on prey or push it to the bottom.	"Gouger" and "swallower." Diet: Reef fish (various species), other sharks, rays.
Mako shark (*Isurus oxyrhinchus*)	Great variety of feeding strategies. Large fish like marlins are bitten so that primarily the tail is injured and the prey cannot swim away.	Hammerhead sharks, other species of ground sharks, cephalopods.

Species	Feeding Strategy	Diet of Adults
Silky shark (*Carcharhinus falciformis*)	Often hunts in groups, often darting into schools of fish.	Primarily "swallower." Diet: Fish (mackerel, cephalopods, etc.), invertebrates such as jellyfish, nautilus, open ocean crabs.
Tiger shark (*Galeocerdo cuvier*)	Usually approaches prey slowly. Often rolls slightly to grab prey, but may also just lift snout and bite.	Most varied diet of all large sharks! Primarily "gouger." Eats live and dead prey. Diet: Fish (variety of reef fish, mackerel, etc.), sharks (dogfish sharks, angle sharks, reef sharks, etc.), rays (stingrays, manta rays, etc.), birds (various species), turtles (various species), sea lions, seals, sea snakes (!), crabs, snails, jellyfish.
Great white shark (*Carcharodon carcharias*)	Various strategies—from sneaking up to fast attacks. Often rolls slightly while biting, but occasionally lifts the snout and bites without rolling. Large prey is often bitten to incapacitate it, so it cannot escape.	"Gouger" and "swallower." Diet: Fish (sardines, tuna, swordfish, herring, etc.), sharks (sand tiger shark, blue sharks, hammerhead sharks, etc.), birds (pelicans, penguins, seagulls, etc.), dolphins, marine mammals (otters, seals, sea lions).
Oceanic whitetip shark (*Carcharhinus longimanus*)	Usually slow approach to bite, can also swim through schools of fish (tuna) with mouth agape—then usually fast—and closes it when prey is inside. This species is also known for biting into larger prey and "sawing off" a piece.	"Gouger" and "swallower." Diet: Fish (tuna, mackerel, barracuda, marlin, etc.), rays, cephalopods, birds (various species), turtles, whale carcasses, trash.

Species	Feeding Strategy	Diet of Adults
Whitetip reef shark (*Triaenodon obesus*)	Often hunts in "packs" and corners prey.	Primarily "swallower." Diet: Mostly reef fish (soldier fish, grunts, surgeon fish, morays, etc.), cephalopods.

species' feeding strategy when interacting with one of its members: on one hand, one can better avoid prey-like behaviors with this knowledge, and on the other hand, one can better understand preferred swim patterns of the animal in question. A minority among sharks, such as whale sharks (*Rhinocodon typus*) and basking sharks (*Cetorhinus maximus*), feed on plankton. These species follow plankton blooms and behave similarly to baleen whales. But it has been shown, especially for whale sharks, that they do not eat plankton exclusively, but also eat small fish if they appear in schools. The designation "plankton eater" is thus not quite correct. There is one significant difference between whale sharks and basking sharks in how they feed. The whale shark actively sucks in plankton-rich water, while the basking shark passively lets it flow through its mouth. Passive filtering means that the shark swims through the water with its mouth open and filters out whatever drifts through its mouth and gills.

In addition to the more typical filter feeders, there are also species where one would not suspect the ability to filter food from the water, such as the blue shark (*Prionace glauca*). This species is also capable of filtering plankton to some limited degree. Blue sharks are typical pelagic sharks of the high seas. Since their preferred prey is not always available, the ability to substitute plankton is an evolutionary adaptation to their environment.

Whenever one tries to interact with whale sharks or even basking sharks, one usually observes a noticeable disinterest in humans. This could be connected to the fact that humans in no way remind them of plankton, their normal diet, or that because they feed near the surface of the water, they are more used to encountering a large variety of objects.

Feeding Behaviors and Body Positions

Sharks can feed in all positions. Depending on the angle of approach (see p. 126), they often turn slightly to one side to be able to continue to see the object with their eyes while biting, if it is not to be swallowed whole. Animals eating at the surface especially show varying behaviors. There are species of shark that will approach an object slowly, then turn slightly to the side, such as great white sharks. Others, such as bull sharks, directly approach the object and simply raise their snout. Others, such as blacktip reef sharks, accelerate shortly before reaching the object and literally ram it. There are also species of shark that prefer not to take prey at the surface, even though they live in shallow water. Nurse sharks often look for prey such as lobsters, which hide in holes to evade predators. These sharks can create strong pressure and suction to bring their prey closer to their mouth. If a lobster is not wedged too deeply into its hiding place, the nurse shark can either suck or "blow" it out. This technique is also used to "peel" mollusks out of their shells.

The suction strategy is also used by predators that sit in waiting for their prey, such as angel sharks (*Squatina* spp.). Angel sharks often hide in the sand, waiting for prey animals to swim past their mouth.

Bull sharks often feed
at the surface.

If this happens, the shark opens its mouth and the resulting suction pulls the prey animal inside.

In connection with feeding behaviors, the jumping of some species of sharks is often discussed, which

#1: A great white shark misses an offered piece of…

#2:…"prey" on its first attempt. It snaps again…

seemingly serves to catch prey. Great white sharks especially show astonishing feats. It can happen that the heavy body of a great white shark that weighs several tons shoots out of the water when attacking prey at the surface, such as seals.

Something similar has also been seen in spinner sharks (*Carcharhinus brevipinna*). These animals will approach a school of fish from below, swim into it vertically while spinning their body—thus their name—and grab fish. Since this can happen very close to the surface, it may occur that in the process, they jump out of the water.

It must be clarified that both these species do not jump actively; they simply do not put the brakes on their movement when they reach the surface, and it becomes a jump when the density of the medium they are in changes.

As already mentioned, actual breaching is not unknown for sharks, if, for example, they want to rid themselves of suckerfish. This behavior has so far only been observed in blacktip reef sharks. However, the assumption that this is not an exception and that

#3: … and trying to catch it…

#4: …once more during the same attack.

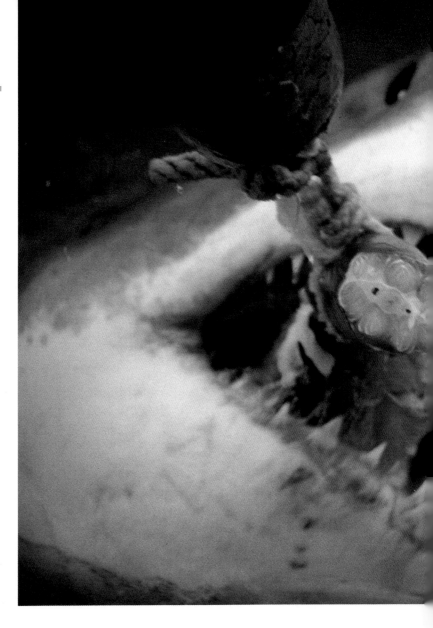

A great white shark is initiating an exploratory bite. Exploratory bites are used to obtain more information about objects. Even though the shark recognizes the prey, the circumstances (prey on a rope) are unfamiliar. Thus the shark grasps the object very carefully and presses it against its palate.

other sharks species may also breach, is certainly justified.

Hunting Strategies

Different strategies for catching prey do not only occur between the different species of sharks, but also

for differently sized sharks of the same species, and
they can even vary for individuals of the same size.

Individual differences may not be blatantly obvious
but lie in the details—such as how one person does not
hold his or her pen in exactly the same way as any
other person, but there are individual differences. It is
important to understand that sharks are not simply
sharks, but individuals, which develop and display

Protrusion of the upper jaw: The upper jaw is only attached to the skull with muscles and therefore very mobile.

individually adapted applications for the same behavior.

In order to understand capturing prey, eating, and the associated strategies, one is best served by observing and analyzing individuals.

This is especially easy for one species, because it catches its prey at the water surface: the great white shark. Great whites change their attack strategies permanently if the goal is successful hunting. It is not rare to observe that after failing to catch their prey with one strategy, they do not only change their swim pattern, but also their speed, to put themselves into an advantageous position. I could observe one animal that used the boat from which the shark bait was hanging for each attempt to grab it. For each attempt it surprised us with a new method—and every time it caught the bait successfully! The animal approached once in the shadow of the boat towards the bait, then from the other side, then it shot out between the two stern motors or even vertically from the blind spot of all observers. Interesting was that the animal—even though it did not know what the boat was—made use of its shape and structure to capture prey. It is beyond doubt that the animal first had to familiarize itself with the body of the boat. But none of us on the boat were aware of this shark, until it first appeared next to the bait.

In order to comprehensively understand the body language of animals, it is urgently necessary to study them when they hunt and eat. Since hunting for prey demands everything of an animal, one usually gets a good impression of its actual capabilities. At least for sharks, it is however not easy to observe them hunting. This is usually only possible when a situation is artificially created, such as offering prey from the stern of boats, which is then filmed.

The more one studies shark body language, the clearer it becomes that seemingly unimportant details, such as the position of the teeth, how far open the mouth is, and visibility of the teeth in the upper jaw play a big role in the attitude (Att) and the behavior. It can easily be seen that a sand tiger shark (*Carcharias taurus*) with its dagger-like pointed teeth uses a more sucking-snapping bite, unlike, for example, a bull

Bull sharks can often be found in very shallow water.

shark, which has more typical shark jaws (dagger-like teeth in the lower jaw, triangular serrated teeth in the upper jaw) and is capable of cutting up prey. This difference results in differing ways of approaching prey.

Thus, one must invest significant time if one is serious about studying sharks. This, of course, is not

only true in regard to the shark's mouth, but also for the eyes, body shape, and color patterns.

When looking at color, it is interesting to understand how a degree of lightness or darkness appears, because this can happen quite fast. In most cases, lightly colored animals of the same shark species tend to stay closer to the water surface than darker colored animals. How long it takes for the color to change has not been studied thoroughly, but it must be assumed that sharks can adjust the color of their skin within one hour.

The more complete one's image of the animal is, the more certain the conclusions that can be drawn after a comparison with the normal appearance of the species, the baseline, for a specific animal. In order to acquire such a baseline, one should, whenever possible, study different individuals of a shark species with different personalities.

Pages 86/87:
Typical appearance of a great white shark while grabbing prey on the surface. Unlike the popular opinion, sharks do not need to roll sideways to grab prey but often will only lift their snout.

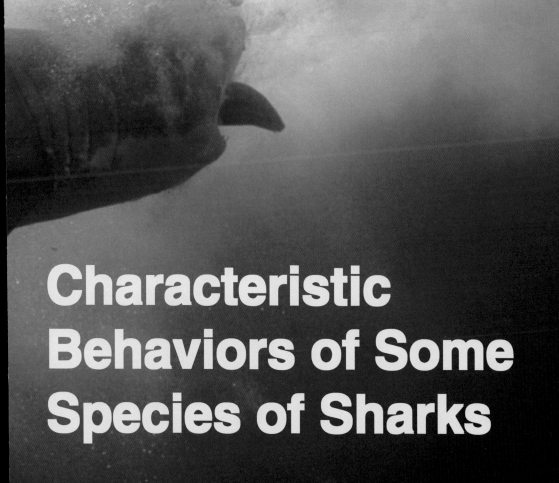

Characteristic Behaviors of Some Species of Sharks

Behavior of Great White Sharks, Bull Sharks, and Reef Sharks

In this chapter, three species of sharks that play a major role in the media are discussed in more detail. These are in particular the great white sharks, which after the movie *Jaws* became the trigger and symbol for mass hysteria surrounding sharks. Also, I want to take a closer look at bull sharks and blacktip reef sharks for the following reasons: Bull sharks are often called the most aggressive near-shore sharks, and blacktip reef sharks cause the most accidents world-wide—more than great white sharks and bull sharks taken together.

The following notes do not comprise a complete treatise about encounters with these species, but only describe selected experiences and impressions. The main emphasis is again on body language and swim patterns.

#1: A great white shark is trying repeatedly to snap...

#2: ...at my shadow on the surface. There may however...

Great White Sharks

If persons work with great white sharks, they will be either snorkeling, free diving, or in scuba gear, when contact is made. If snorkeling, one is to remain at the water surface, and the animals are either encountered below or at the same level.

If the encounter takes place at the water surface, the factor Environment (abbreviated "Env" in the interaction model; see p. 144) is of utmost importance. When diving in deeper water, this is less the case, since the midwater space is less limited than the surface, and the animals always have the option of swimming above the person.

Working at the water surface has advantages and disadvantages: on one hand it limits the options for the animal to flee, on the other hand, the human is in

Encounters at the Water Surface

#3. ...be other reasons for this behavior, which...

#4: ... is also called repetitive aerial gaping (RAG).

A great white shark is chasing a bag filled with crushed fish. That there are no visual clues does not matter since the scent is triggering a strong reaction.

the most common setting for prey. In the latter there is also an advantage: It is actually possible to encounter great white sharks at the water surface, and interact with them, because one is very interesting to the shark, and the animal usually approaches very closely (Warning! Do not imitate this! Sharks are predators!). For our work, we must understand how the animals try to assess us—this is why we assign great significance to positioning the prey. Since only a few aspects of our behavior (for example, our position, changes in water pressure through fin movement, swim pattern, etc.) match up with patterns that are familiar patterns to the animals, a shark must at first approach carefully. This slow approach allows the human time for observation, and almost always guarantees that the animal will employ a variety of swim patterns in order to better classify the situation. This means in turn, that one can obtain a good idea of the animal's

A great white shark is sticking its head out of the water to check out a person. It is assumed that this behavior is similar to that of swordfish.

motivation based on its body language during this phase.

In most cases, a great white shark is seen either passing by or patrolling along the periphery. When an animal passes by, it usually approaches in such a way that it does not need to change direction to disappear from the field of vision of the observer. For the shark, the advantage of "just passing by" is that it does not encounter a direct obstacle during this first approach, and it can swim "through the setting" and disappear. Its direction of approach is not chosen randomly, but the result of previous scouting. Scouting usually takes place at a distance where it is unlikely to be noticed at all, unless it approached directly below the water surface.

Passive Approach

When I interact with a great white shark, I usually choose a passive approach first. As explained earlier, one should give the animal time to assess the situation, and use this time in turn to observe the animal and study its swim patterns and various behaviors as much as they can be recognized. One must always understand that sharks do not know who or what

Seals are very agile and no easy prey for great white sharks.

humans are, and that they use their senses together with swim patterns to get more information about the foreign object.

Exploratory Bite

When interacting with great white sharks one thing must always be kept in mind: the animal is not planning to injure the human, but only "wants to understand" what or who the object in its vicinity is. This does not necessarily mean that a great white will use an exploratory bite to answer this question conclusively. In most cases, the animal will turn away first. In my experience, most animals only want to determine from a certain distance what this unknown object is. Most of them do not come very close, and even fewer bite—this inhibition threshold is rarely crossed.

Should, however, an exploratory bite be used, the shark can find out additional details about the

Great white sharks prefer to attack the fins of seals, rendering them unable to escape.

unknown object or human with the sense organs in its palate—information that it cannot get from its other sense organs. Even when it is clear that the shark will bite, this does not have to be fast or violent, but rather restrained. If a great white shark intends to use an exploratory bite, it usually approaches the human very slowly and sniffs the individual first. Only once have I experienced an animal that approached fast and used an exploratory bite. And because this usually happens so hesitantly, it is possible for the human to control the situation. The sniffing shark is pushed away gently and without violence. I am well aware that most people will panic at this point and would react in the wrong way, and few people would seek out such close contact to a great white shark as I did and will con-tinue to do. But interactions with great white sharks are possible—and I have experienced them many times. From these encounters I could find out, what one can, must, and should do in these situations.

When interacting with great white sharks, one must let go of the idea that this animal has anything to do with the animals portrayed in *Jaws*. It is only an animal that wants to find out who or what we are.

Frontal Approach

When passing by, a shark can only obtain limited information. Sooner or later it will change to a frontal approach pattern (see p. 40) to find out whether the object, or the person, will react like potential prey. Such would be moving away from the shark, that is, to retreat in the direction in which the shark is swimming (the typical traffic accident syndrome in movies—

Penguins are not a preferred food of great white sharks. These birds still choose to stay in groups for increased protection.

a person runs away from a car on the road in the direction in which the car is driving). This reaction would confirm to the animal what it is trying to find out and what it is "hoping" to find. When a shark approaches from the front, one must either remain in place or move away to the side. A reaction that does not match a prey pattern will suggest to the animal that the object in front of it is not prey. This does not mean that the shark will immediately give up its attempts. But now it has to choose a new strategy. A change of strategy also means that other sense organs must be used.

In order to attract great white sharks, one can attach kelp to a string. Since great whites "know" that kelp usually drifts with the current, they will investigate it if it does not. Often they will lightly bite the kelp or bump it with their nose.

In most cases, a frontal approach will become a lateral approach (see p. 41), which allows the shark to use its lateral line system. When great white sharks display this approach pattern from the side, one must stop moving, because the shark will approach very closely in order to sense changes in water pressure. These pressure changes are probably the only thing that a

Approach from the Side

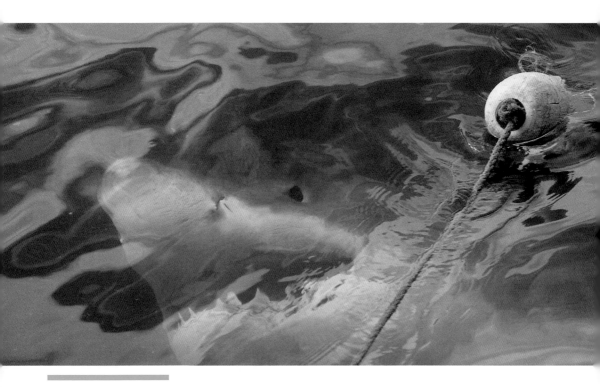

A great white shark is focusing on the shadow of a person on the water surface. The bait is often ignored in this case. A reason may be that the animal first examines the unknown object before dealing with the known.

human produces that fits into the trigger patterns of a shark and that is familiar from the movements of a seal or fish. Whatever moves in the water creates changes in water pressure—more so if it is fleeing!

When I enter into interaction with a great white shark, I usually do not move at all, but every so often I have to move my hands or fin-covered feet in order to maintain my position, since there it is often a light current in the water according to the environment ("Env" from ADORE, see p. 144). The shark will then concentrate on these movements. Once fin or arm movements have attracted its full attention, it is not always easy to keep the animal at a distance. But this is not necessary. The animal is not going to suddenly change its strategy, shoot forward, and bite the human, but will continue to move slowly. The major focus for the interacting human remains in analyzing the shark's body language.

When a shark approaches a person, one should take time to study it. One of the most noticeable features of its appearance is certainly the fixed position of the jaw and the movement of the eyes. These eye-catching features should not distract from observing the whole animal (attitude (Att) in the interaction model, see p. 149). When the shark is very close, one has a tendency to forget to look at the obvious, such as fin positions. It is also important to observe the angle of approach, as well as the "threatening angle" if one is moving. Especially if the distance is very short, one must remember that this closeness is also very stressful for the animal. It is absolutely possible that the shark will suddenly disappear. Because the amount of information may be too voluminous, and the shark may not be able to filter it sufficiently, it may under those circumstances simply swim off. However, this is rare if a person is in the water, but it usually happens when the animal has approached a boat, since this object is much larger. The many unknown stimuli that originate from the boat, especially after a tempting piece of bait has "called," could trigger such a stress reaction in the animal.

A great white shark is following the scent and food particles from a bag of food. Great whites, like most other species of shark, require a current to find the source of a scent. They notice a scent, position themselves into the current, and swim against it towards the source.

In very rare cases we encountered great white sharks that did not limit themselves to interaction at a distance but touched us intentionally. This happened either with the snouts, or—very hesitantly—with the mouth.

Encounters in Midwater or at the Bottom

If one does not use a snorkel but compressed air to dive, it can be observed that sharks react strongly to the sounds of breathing, so that the use of rebreathers (closed-circuit breathing systems for scuba divers, where no air is exhaled into the water, but the air is reprocessed; they do not make as much noise as the more common compressed air breathing systems) is recommended. If such an apparatus is not available, one should stop breathing when a shark approaches. This is not exactly pleasant, but is the only way to prevent the shark from turning away prematurely because of the noise.

Especially when working in scuba gear—not staying at the water surface, but descending into midwater or even to the bottom—one will notice with surprise

#1: A great white shark observes a person…

#2: … on a boat. All of this happens…

that the sharks will adjust to the position of the diver immediately. Rarely, the animal will swim above the person, because observed from above, the diver does not stand out against the dark bottom. The shark is possibly trying to avoid putting itself into a "prey position." Whether a great white shark is capable of recognizing a seeming subordination in an unknown object—even though there seems to be a general indication that this may be the case—remains an open question at the current state of knowledge.

Great white sharks prefer to swim in two locations: either directly below the water surface or just above the bottom. That an animal swimming close to the bottom can not be seen easily and is difficult to interact with, does not require detailed explanation. If a diver encounters an animal at the bottom, it is recommended, that he or she also descend and stay at the bottom. A shark swimming near the bottom will have fewer flight paths available, since it cannot dive down. This will affect the approach behavior of the shark,

Preferred Swimming Locations

#3: … very quickly. Great whites are able to stay upright…

#4: … and motionless at the water surface.

since the animal can only pass by the diver on the side or above, which puts it in an inferior and disadvantageous position.

Bull Sharks

Bull sharks are typical shallow water sharks. They often swim into river deltas or even up rivers, and they can show up in pure freshwater miles away from the ocean. Basically, these animals are as harmless as other shark species. The relatively large number of accidents involving bull sharks, when compared to all worldwide shark incidents, occurs because they often move into river deltas, which offer much food but have bad visibility. (About 70 to 100 shark accidents happen worldwide every year, where bull sharks are involved in 10 to 15 accidents. Since not all accidents are investigated sufficiently to determine the involved species, it is possible that the number of incidents involving

Most species of sharks are of a color that allows them to blend in with their environment.

bull sharks is higher.) In river deltas the food density is rather high, since the plankton that is floating down the river dies off when it reaches brackish water, which attracts animals that eat it. At the top of this food chain are sharks in general, and bull sharks specifically.

In waters that teem with so much life and floating particles, a large number of stimuli reach the bull sharks. They filter them and are forced to ignore some, so that they are probably in a higher state of alertness. They take in olfactory and acoustic signals from their prey, but are also exposed to many stimuli that are produced by other organisms, which also hunt and feed in the same area.

Bull sharks, as well as other sharks, often feed at the surface, if there is prey there.

Contrary to the common view, sharks often swim into very shallow water—sometimes even into freshwater rivers.

If in this extreme case of overstimulation a human is added, which causes pressure changes in the water and turbulence, a confrontation seems practically unavoidable. In these areas of the river, bull sharks are exposed to higher levels of stress because they are subjected to so many stimuli that do not exist in the ocean. Maybe this is the reason why accidents are so common here.

The "Inner Circle"

Bull sharks generally come close to objects or people, because their inner circle has a rather small radius. If one does not know this, this, of course, seems threatening. In addition, by human standards, the small eyes of bull sharks seem frightening. These eyes, however, are an adaptation to living in shallow, bright shore areas.

Since bull sharks prefer to swim in shallow water—and most interaction with them takes place there—their options for flight are often limited, because their small "inner circle" (their individual space, see p. 35) usually touches the water surface or the bottom. I have repeatedly observed that the flight reactions of bull sharks seem limited when their inner circle touches the water surface.

Why bull sharks have a significantly smaller than expected inner circle cannot be determined conclusively. Even though the lateral line system plays a significant role in relation to the size of this space, especially in bull sharks—but also the previously described great white sharks—other factors seem to be important. These other factors may even be more important than the lateral line system; what these factors are is currently unknown. In addition, we also

Two bull sharks are fighting over one piece of food.

The eyes of a bull shark are rolled back temporarily as soon as they get into contact with air (reduced pressure compared to water).

Contrary to the common view, sharks will feed when an opportunity arises, not at certain times of the day.

do not know enough about what must happen for a shark—such as a bull shark or great white shark—to violate this threshold of the inner circle and come closer to an unknown object.

As long as humans do not move in the presence of sharks, there is no real danger.

Working with bull sharks shows clearly how low their threshold towards other species is, and that they approach quite closely after a short time. Not uncommonly, there is physical contact with the human. Such

Encounters in Shallow Water

touching has absolutely nothing (!) to do with a shark accident, but can simply be attributed to the fact that bull sharks, because of the limitations imposed on movement and avoidance in shallow water, easily touch things. Such contacts are more a consequence of the special situation in shallow water than intentional actions of the shark.

Because in shallow waters one is usually snorkeling or swimming, the bull sharks usually appear immediately below or to the side; the arm and leg movements of the person play a decisive role here. It is necessary and very important that one not move the limbs at all or only minimally when bull sharks are in the vicinity. If an animal approaches anyway, in order to take a closer look at hands or feet, one should allow this. The animal will most certainly not (!) bite immediately to obtain additional information (exploratory bite, see p. 92). It is much more likely that the movement as such, and the changes in water pressures caused by it, trigger an increased interest of the shark. The shark may try to use its thermal and electric sensory organs to gather more information about the

#1: Interaction between human and shark: …

#2: A bull shark is showing typical jostling behavior…

limbs. This is only possible if the animal comes very close.

I often have had a bull shark directly at my feet, fins, or hands, and one of the first lessons that I learned was to pull my arms and legs slowly (!) away from the animal. A quick movement suggests—at least in terms of the resulting changes in water pressure—a prey item.

If the bull sharks are so close that one must touch them, because one feels threatened and wants to push them away, it is actually not dangerous to touch the animal on the head (not near the mouth!) to direct it to turn around or in a different direction. Without doubt, it is not everybody's cup of tea to seek out physical contact with sharks or even bull sharks, but this actually has the desired result. The same result can be accomplished—with a somewhat smaller success rate—by pushing water towards the head (eyes and gill areas). The water movement and increased pressure on the body suggests to the animal that it is being approached. This rarely happens to a large predator and usually only with other sharks. In such situations,

#3: ... for a close-up investigation...

#4: ... of the object—a diver.

one can see how the shark slightly turns away its head and adjusts its direction of swimming.

Reef Sharks: The Blacktip Reef Shark

An object approaches the "inner circle" of this Caribbean reef shark: The right pectoral fin is already pressed down slightly, and the animal will veer off to the right.

There are about 30 species of sharks in the genus *Carcharhinus*. Blacktip reef sharks are usually no longer than 1.5 m, live in all the oceans of the world, and inhabit shallow water zones as well as the open water above the continental shelf and around islands. There is one big difference to the other *Carcharhinus* sharks: Blacktip reef sharks cause the most accidents worldwide. In Florida, the state with by far the most

Several blacktip sharks and Caribbean reef sharks are attempting to take away food from each other. Such situations are often called "feeding frenzies," where sharks are said to bite blindly and injure each other. This is a wrong interpretation: Slow motion video recordings show that this turmoil is quite under control and no animals are injured.

reported accidents annually (between 30 and 40), they are responsible for about 90% of all accidents.

Do they have a particularly low inhibition threshold towards unknown objects? This is certainly one of the reasons. Another one is the fact that in their area of distribution, a lot of water sports and sport fishing takes place. This causes frequent encounters between humans and blacktip reef sharks attracted by bait. The bait is not put out for sharks, but for fish, but the sharks are also attracted.

Curiosity

Blacktip reef sharks, like other members of *Carcharhinus*, are very curious. This could be related to the fact that these animals usually swim in schools, and the more animals patrol a feeding area, the larger the competition for each individual. They seem proportionally more interested in new objects. Unlike the general opinion, sharks do not limit their feeding

Female Caribbean reef shark with bite marks (belly, at edge of photograph) from a male during mating season.

Pages 112/113: Sharks often have bite marks from other sharks on their body or head. Such bites can have various origins; usually, they are acquired during feeding or mating. In this case, the scratches on the snout are related to feeding.

to certain times of the day, but will eat whenever they find something edible. Because anything potentially unknown theoretically is food to them, it must be assumed that their inhibition threshold for exploring new objects is lowered when the animals are in groups.

It could therefore be a necessary part of their behavior spectrum to have fewer inhibitions towards strange objects and approach them relatively fast. My own experiences point in this direction: Often I jumped from a boat into the water without seeing a single blacktip reef shark—but not a minute passed and three or four animals showed up in proximity.

Like great white sharks and bull sharks, blacktip reef sharks have a relatively small inner circle—as mentioned earlier, in all species "small" refers to the size relative to their body size. Blacktip reef sharks are one of the easiest to read sharks in regard to their intentions, because their interactions are usually goal oriented. Because they are not very large and swim relatively fast, their "fin language" is usually easy to interpret. Since they usually approach quickly, the various behaviors, such as apparent or real rolling of the eyes, can be distinguished.

The Inner Circle

The often described "feeding frenzies" are in reality well-organized and fast-paced sequences of actions in the context of feeding hierarchies.

Encounters between Sharks and Humans

A great white shark is following a "cookie." Unnatural objects floating at the surface are often investigated with great interest by these animals.

Signals and Communication

In the last few chapters, various aspects of the body language of sharks were discussed, with the goal of correctly interpreting movements and behaviors. In addition, there are a number of additional signals that sharks send more or less continuously, and with which they communicate their intentions. Such signals can be minimal and unobtrusive, such as a barely notice-able change in swimming direction, a minute change in color, or a slight change in how wide the mouth is opened. As soon as such signals are registered and responded to by other sharks, that is, they simply react, communication between the animals is established.

Sharks communicate with each other. They not only communicate among themselves, but also with their prey. In general, one can say that communication takes place when one animal reacts to the signals produced by another animal.

Signal Filtering

A shark cannot always react immediately to the signals from another shark, since the animal must set priorities. For example, a shark discovers food at the same time as another shark at a distance, the latter indicating clearly that it is also claiming the food. Suddenly, a human appears from another direction into this situation. Now the shark has to deal with the fact that another shark is competing with him for the food, and that there is potential danger from the diver. The latter is assumed, because humans are unknown beings to sharks. Because we are relatively large—in most cases larger than the shark—we are at first considered potential threats. It is conceivable that, in addition, a suckerfish has attached to the lateral line of a shark, which falsifies its perception of the water pressure. In such a case, the shark must weigh all these different factors and come to a decision. This example is meant to show how many and which signals can all affect a shark at the same time. It shows that the animal cannot simply react to the signals from the other shark, but that other signals play a role too and must be processed and responded to.

This weighing of factors is also called filtering, where the shark puts aside everything that is not required or is less important to resolve the current situation. In our example, the one factor that is not likely to be filtered out in the final analysis is the diver, who is preventing the shark from obtaining its food. Therefore, the shark will feed, swim away, or start to find out more about the diver and interact with him or her. This is because the other shark, the prey, and the suckerfish are known objects to the shark. The following scenario is possible: Our shark could fight with the other shark over the food—an everyday occurrence. But the diver is unknown and also close to the source of food, so he or she might also be interested in the food. The unknown diver is also a potential threat to the shark. Therefore, our shark cannot turn its attention to the other shark or the food, but first has to deal with the unknown. Only after the unknown has either been understood or has disappeared, can the animal return to the situations that are known and familiar.

In the above described scenario, one would see behaviors in the shark that seem to make sense, as well as behaviors that appear nonsensical (displacement activities), since the animal is torn between several possible reactions. I have observed animals in similar situations, and they ended up circling in place, keeping the same distance to me and the other objects. As soon as I retreated a little, circling stopped, and the animal focused on the other aspects of the situation.

If as a human one is capable of correctly decoding and interpreting such situations, one can understand them and recognize that sharks, like other animals, are influenced by many factors and can consider them all in order to react appropriately. Observation of the surrounding area is an important factor when judging a situation, but it requires some experience.

How Signals Arise

In the above example, it was very likely that the shark in question sent signals not only to the other shark, but also to the diver, to tell everybody that he was not happy with the situation and felt uncomfortable (at least in his world). This was expressed by the circling. Since I knew how to properly interpret the circling in this situation, I could relieve the shark's stress, and it could go on and deal with other things.

Sharks communicate in many ways with each other, and depending on their surroundings, this works better or worse. For example, the signal "slight opening of the mouth" is barely recognizable in murky water, while a corresponding swim pattern that uses the whole body can still be seen and recognized. Therefore, it is really very important that one also observes the signals that the sharks use to communicate with each other (!) when interacting with them. If

one has become familiar with a signal or behavior, one can learn to understand its application. For example, it matters how strongly it is expressed, how long it lasts, and how often it is repeated.

The environment also plays an important role ("Env" in the interaction model, see page 144), since the choice of signal and the capability of the recipient to correctly interpret it depend on it. A signal in clear water is easily visible, but near a dark background, such as a reef or at dusk, this can be difficult.

If we relate the above to sharks that communicate with humans, a large problem becomes apparent. The shark can employ the whole repertoire of communication

A male bull shark is patrolling close to the bottom. Even though the animal seems to be looking in a different direction, it is aware of the presence of the person.

Communicating with Humans

Snorklers and sharks can safely interact if certain rules are observed.

signals that it uses with other sharks or other ocean dwellers, but it will realize soon that there is not much of a response, that the recipient—that is the human—is not reacting appropriately. Therefore, when encountering a shark, one must try to fulfill the shark's expectations with one's reactions. This requires experiments that must be performed under comparable conditions, and by means of them it can be discovered how a shark reacts to the signals sent by humans.

Signals that are always understood by sharks are size (broadside), approach angle (relative to the animal), and changes in water pressure, etc. If, for example, a shark clearly displays stress behaviors and excitedly swims around a source of food, it seems likely that the animal is signaling to the close-by human that it should retreat. The appropriate answer of the human to this displayed behavior of the shark would be to withdraw.

Of course, sharks have a much more specific language and a differentiated range of signals than we could even come close to decoding. But, each correct instance of communication, even if it is minimal and rudimentary, helps. Even if one knows *how* the animals communicate with each other or how they react, *what* one communicates to a shark by choosing a certain approach angle or other behavior may not be clear. To find an answer to this takes much time. One must create situations where humans try to imitate what a shark just did and analyze its reactions. One must always keep in mind that the seemingly same response signal—seen in the shark—may have a different meaning when executed by another kind of being, such as a human.

We will never be able to completely decode the language of sharks, but I'm completely convinced that we can learn behaviors and reactions that will create a positive reaction from the shark for continuing the interaction.

Interactions between Sharks and Humans

Even though the topic "interaction with sharks," that is, relating to and communicating of sharks with humans, is a rather recent area of research, it is important to publish these first results to a large audience. Any knowledge about shark behaviors should be made available to people who, because of their profession or recreational activities, such as scuba diving or snorkeling, come into contact with

A snorkler interacting with a shark.

Result of great white shark tourism: Often boats are crammed full with dive tourists in order to show them great white sharks. The focus is on quick money, not the well-being of the animals, and the tourists will not experience natural shark behavior.

sharks, and anybody else who is interested. This includes depicting sharks in the media how they really are. Sharks continue to be labeled monsters, especially of course great whites, bull, and tiger sharks.

In recent years, dive tourism with sharks, similar to whale watching, has significantly increased. The underlying idea is certainly good, but it also has its negative aspects. One of the most negative consequences is that with this kind of tourism, the animal is not in the foreground, but only how fascination with fear of sharks can be exploited for profit. I find this kind of shark commercialization despicable.

Important and worthy of support, in my opinion, is ecotourism, which allows people to experience animals as they really are, where the focus is actually on the shark. This kind of tourism makes shark encounters possible where an interaction can take place. The organizers of this kind of dive tourism are aware of their responsibility for the animals and are advocates for them.

Unfortunately, this responsible shark tourism is not yet widely practiced. Most providers of shark diving trips have obviously not yet understood that the relationship between sharks and humans must not be completely one-sided. It must not be limited to attracting and admiring the animals. It is absolutely possible—and this should also be done!—to "communicate" with the animals and actively (!) interact with them. Each diver should be given this opportunity during shark encounters, so that they can question, revise, or confirm their opinions.

With this type of shark encounter, an ecologically oriented tourism can become an essential component of environmental protection in general, and wildlife protection in particular. The key to interacting with sharks and other animals is their body language.

In order to change the public image of the shark as a killer monster, it is not sufficient to enable a limited number of tourists to have such shark encounters. To really understand these animals requires saying

Ecotourism must go hand in hand with information about these animals in order to increase understanding.

goodbye to thinking "inside the box" and the distinction between "nice" and "dangerous evil" sharks. Many divers have successfully interacted with reef sharks—and that, in spite of the general opinion that it is not possible to interact with them.

Behavior researchers therefore also have to work with these seemingly dangerous sharks and show that analysis and interpretation of shark body language is the same for all species. Interaction with a great white shark or a bull shark is in no way more dangerous or unpredictable than interaction with other shark species. In spite of all the wrong information in people's heads, these large sharks behave in exactly the same way as the shark species that are considered harmless. If this is kept in mind, one can recognize that these supposed monsters are simply misunderstood.

Creation of the ADORE-SANE Interaction Model

The ADORE-SANE Interaction Model

When sharks approach they can only do this at the same level, above, or below the human.

It took about 10 years for the following described concept for interacting with sharks to be worked out in its current form. Even though the animals did not come into contact with humans earlier, it took until the beginning of the 1990s for me to realize that interaction between humans and sharks is not a mixture of random behaviors, but that the animals contemplate each situation, are influenced by varying environmental factors, and—probably most important—react to the activities of the observer.

I remember well a milestone encounter with bull sharks in Walker's Cay, Bahamas, which for the first time brought to my attention that sharks analyze a situation and show a reaction specific to humans.

Bull sharks have a bulky body. They are large, broad-snouted, and have extremely small eyes. These eyes in particular seem to catch the attention of the

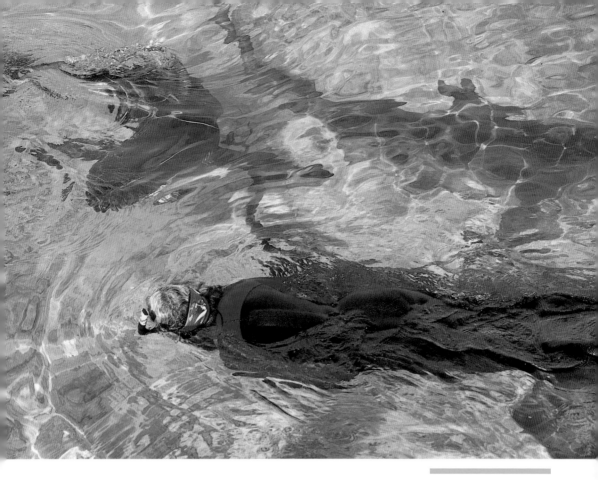

observer. The following lines are an abbreviated excerpt from my German book "Das Laecheln der Haie" ("The Smile of Sharks"), which describe a situation where we tossed bait into the water. This made a splashing sound each time. The following scene developed:

Well-trained ecotourists can interact with bull sharks without problems.

The bull shark pulls some maneuvers before he drives away the lemon shark for the first time. But a lemon shark cannot in any way be compared to a nurse shark, it will return to the scene after a few minutes. The situation seems to get more interesting and we [Note: Doug Perrine and I] are waiting to see what might happen next, somehow forgetting that we are both in the water, and that no more splashes are created [Note: the splashes were caused by the falling pieces of bait].

The dorsal fin of a shark is "cutting" through the water, as often depicted in cartoons.

And the bull shark is circling. Suddenly, I have a feeling that the bull shark realizes who is responsible for the splashes and that it is more and more interested in us, because otherwise there is nothing else in the water that could hold its attention.... Suddenly, it turns around and swims directly toward us. One jump and I find out instantly how one can walk on water in fins. I land and look around, and who is already standing next to me? I believe that he too has used this method of walking for the first time today. We look at each other and understand without words. With this guy (the bull shark) it will be a little difficult, but Doug requires a photograph. We return to the water and quickly run back across the water again. Back in the water, back on the land. We become well-practiced water runners, but visibly frustrated ones. Already two hours have gone by with us rushing back and forth, and Doug has not taken a single photograph. I have to stop because I still have a class to teach, and go on my way. Doug remains for another hour, and when I ask him in the evening, he only says: "In the water, out of the water, in the water..." Well maybe we will be luckier later. Doug tries again during the next two days, but in vain. I return to the rock several times and see the bull shark almost every day. It almost seems as if it was making fun of us...

It took a long time for me to truly understand what had happened then. Only much later I realized that the shark did not want to bite me, but simply wanted to get a closer look and understand. I showed up in its world, and it connected me in some way with the food or the lack thereof. Today I know, because over the years I have often found myself in the same situation—and did not run across the water as I did then, but gave the animal time to "explain," that is, to interpret the situation.

Over the years, I interacted with many sharks of many different species and observed each dive or snorkel outing as a separate event: one shark did this or that in a certain situation, it reacted this way or that. I collected more dives, piles of report sheets, and more and more I realized that the various species of shark approach humans similarly in certain situations and behave in similar ways. It became clear that these interactions between sharks and humans should be

Bull sharks often approach frontally to get an object to react; its reaction shall provide more information.

considered from two angles: first from the point of view of the shark, and second from the point of view of the person, be it a diver, swimmer, or snorkler.

I started to work out similarities between the various situations and differences that were triggered by the conditions. One step at a time, a model developed, which became the start of considering an encounter with a shark as a possibility. After the first working hypotheses had been established, I began to analyze old situations from a fresh viewpoint (including the encounter with the bull shark described above), but also started to interact with sharks in a way that was necessary to test the model.

Finally, five factors that have to be taken into account when interacting with sharks, and four factors that are important from the human side, were singled out and named. I call this interaction model ADORE-SANE, where the first five letters stand for factors concerning the shark, and the last four letters stand for factors concerning the interacting human. The original names are in English since I discussed the model primarily with English-speaking people. ADORE = Attitude, Direction, Origin, Relation, Environment. SANE = Situation, Activity, Nervousness, Experience.

Angle of Approach or Threatening Angle

In addition, the shark can only swim directly towards the person, or swim past at an angle that is smaller than 90°. This angle is formed by an imaginary line between the observer and the shark (line of sight) and a second line that extends from the longitudinal axis of the shark's body. It is called "angle of approach" or "threatening angle." It is called "angle of approach" when the interacting human is motionless, expecting the shark to approach (that is, the human is not moving), and "threatening angle" when the human actively swims towards the shark.

If a shark approaches frontally, it can usually be

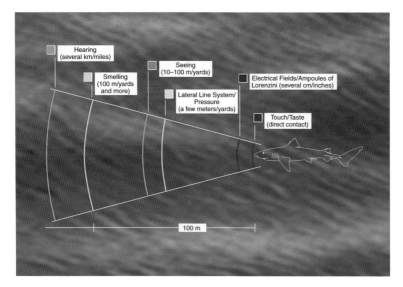

Graphical representation of shark senses and the distance at which they can be used.

seen from quite a distance; if it approaches from behind, one can only see it by turning the head or turning around. If one sees a shark in the water ahead, one can at least see the head (if the shark approaches exactly from the front) or maximally the whole animal from the side. In the first case, the animal is swimming

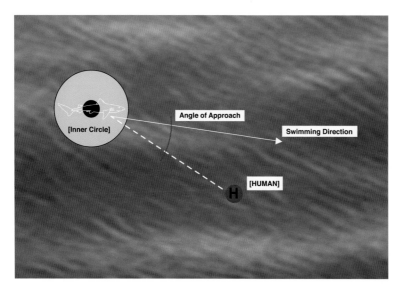

The angle of approach is the angle between the direction in which the shark is swimming (shown as an unbroken white line) and a line (dotted) from the shark to the human.

An object is at the edge of the "inner circle" of this male Caribbean reef shark; the right pectoral fin, which is slightly pressing down, indicates this.

directly towards the person. If its side is visible (in which case the animal swims along at an angle of about 90° to the observing human), it will simply continue to swim. If the angle is less than 90°, the animal is swimming in some way in the person's direction. If the angle is significantly smaller, the animal will get closer. And if the angle is zero, the shark is swimming directly towards me. These are the different

directions in which a shark can approach a human.

It now seems obvious that a cautious shark will approach at a larger angle than a bolder animal, which will approach more or less directly. A cautious shark will not swim above the person, because it will lose several advantages by doing that. When a cautious shark approaches from the front, it usually does it at a relatively large angle in relationship to the human and swims, whenever possible, below him or her. It is rare that a shark approaches a human directly, almost always it will do so at least at a small angle. The size of the angle depends on two factors: the inner circle and the outer circle, which are explained below.

The inner and outer circles are not actually circles, but really spherical zones that surround a shark in its three-dimensional ocean habitat, and at whose center is the shark itself.

"Inner Circle" And "Outer Circle"

One can imagine the following: The shark is inside these imaginary spheres. As soon as its boundaries are touched by a living being, a reaction is triggered. We have a similar concept and experience with "personal space," which can also be imagined as a sphere surrounding us. We start to become uncomfortable if someone approaches too near or even invades our space. We only allow familiar people to come very close. The same seems to be the case for sharks. The inner sphere can be compared to our personal distance; the outer sphere can be considered the area of first perception or a "circle of attention." When sharks swim and notice an object at a distance, they usually change their direction slightly. When the shark first reacts to it, the object is on the surface of the outer sphere, that is, the outer circle. Sharks will pass by an object at a distance in such a way that their personal distance (the inner sphere, that is, the inner circle) does not touch it. The reason why one usually talks not of spheres but circles is because humans look at an animal in a straight line and are therefore on the same plane (line of sight).

The area between the inner and outer circle is called "interzone." This is where most interactions between sharks and humans take place.

However, as mentioned earlier, it is possible that one cannot see the shark or only notices it when one turns around and the shark is already directly at one's back. It is assumed that a shark can consciously and intentionally approach in this way and express a different motivation from an animal that approaches from the front. The position where the human first notices the shark is called "origin." It is the first eye contact between human and shark. The term "origin" gains a different weight, if one only becomes aware of the approaching animal when it is directly at one's back.

The Five Concepts of ADORE

With the three aspects "direction," "spatial relationship," and "origin" one can already analyze a shark during the first phase of an encounter. These three terms are abbreviated in English to D (Direction), R (Relation), and O (Origin), and contain the DOR part of ADORE. The other two letters stand for Attitude (Att),

where the external attitude and appearence of the animal is meant, and Environment (Env). These terms and their meanings are discussed in detail later (see p. 135 ff.).

This much for now: For an untrained diver or a diver unfamiliar with sharks, it is difficult to interpret Attitude. It is better that he or she ignore this factor and focus particularly on the Environment. The environment affects a living being quite strongly: it is easy to see how a shark will approach a human very

Kelp forests are home to many species of sharks.

More and more films
document what sharks
are really like. No
cages are used during
filming.

differently in a murky canal, the open ocean, or along
the edge of a reef. The environment not only includes
the structure of the underwater landscape. But also
includes other environmental elements, such as dive
boats, anchor chains, and other divers—that is, everything, that in any way affects the interaction between
shark and human.

Interpreting the appearance of a shark is, as previously said, not easy. There are (rare) situations, when
it is obvious to anybody what mood the shark is in. If,
for example, there is a hook in the shark's mouth, and
maybe a trailing rope, and the animal twists left and
right while approaching, anybody can recognize that

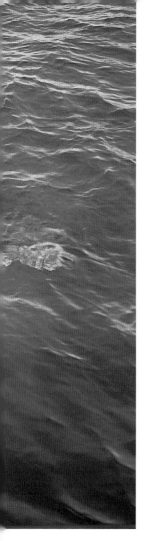

this shark is not feeling well, and that these exaggerated movements are not triggered by the diver but by the hook and line. It gets more complicated when nothing obvious influences the movement pattern or appearance of the shark. Different appearances will be discussed in more detail later.

As explained above, the first part of this model (ADORE) refers to the shark. The second part (SANE) refers exclusively to humans. In the same way as in the first part of the model's name, these four letters also stand for four concepts: S is for Situation, A is for Activity, N is for Nervousness and E for Experience.

The Four
Concepts of
SANE

At first contact with a shark, a decisive factor for how the encounter will proceed seems to be how a person is moving, that is, in what activity is he or she involved. Sharks are primarily attracted by certain types of movements and the sounds connected to them. It makes a difference whether a person splashes around at the surface, free dives, is spear fishing, snorkeling, or scuba diving, or just slaps the surface of the water. In addition, the behavior of a shark is also influenced by the situation itself. The following scenarios are conceivable: A person is floating at the surface of the water and suddenly realizes that he or she is drifting off. Frightened, the swimmer tries to reach the shore. Or, a diver jumps into the water, loses his or her weight belt while preparing the camera for underwater photography—and is drifting on the surface. These and similar situations affect and change the degree of nervousness of a person, and this can—if sharks are in the picture—trigger reactions. Nervousness in the ADORE-SANE model can also be understood as the general emotional state of a person. It describes how a person feels generally when handling a situation, that is, how stressful a given situation is.

The degree of nervousness is also influenced by a person's past experiences. An experienced diver, who may have encountered many different situations, will react in a more relaxed manner than a person with little or no experience. Even though SANE (Situation, Activity, Nervousness, Experience) is rarely considered consciously when an encounter or interaction with a shark is in progress, these four factors precisely decide how a shark will ultimately approach a person.

ADORE-SANE is a flexible model that can be used in a variety of ways. For example, one can focus on the approach direction or the environment, or focus exclusively on animals that are near the inner circle.

The main purpose, however, is to analyze and understand a situation that involves a shark in its entirety. One limitation must be pointed out: In the same way as there are different situations when scuba diving, snorkeling, or surfing, representatives of the same shark species may react differently in the same situation. When the model is used, one must always consider that sharks are individuals, like humans. This means, that each shark shows individual deviations from the typical species behavior, and that the behavior patterns of individuals of a species can be expressed differently.

Characteristics of the Concepts of ADORE-SANE

Even though I have now explained the basic aspects of the model, I would like to list all nine concepts of ADORE-SANE separately and describe their significance in more depth.

The first five concepts (ADORE) refer to the shark. They inform about the situation and state in which the shark is.

ADORE

Attitude is the only aspect of ADORE where a certain amount of experience with sharks is an advantage. But even without experience one can almost always judge the attitude of a shark correctly. It is important not to focus on instant assessment of the animal, but to observe it for a few seconds. As described on p. 44, one should get a feel for the speed of the animal. This is done by counting tail beats per time unit. If one notices that the frequency does not change, one can then focus on the question of where one is located in respect to the outer and inner circles of the animal (see p. 129). Pectoral fins that are pressed down are an indicator that one is close to the boundary of the inner circle. If the shark is farther away than the perimeter of its inner circle, and its pectoral fins are still pressed down, one should check whether the animal is hunching (see p. 51). Depending on the distance to the shark, that is, its inner circle, behaviors such as turning of the head, rolling of the eyes, and others (see p. 23) can be interpreted correctly.

Att (Attitude)

Attitude is also strongly influenced by the environment. It is therefore advisable for a diver to consider the conditions underwater before embarking on a dive.

Sharks, like scuba divers, are affected by the

In order to observe feeding behavior from a close distance, bull sharks are often fed close-up by snorklers. This situation is controllable, as long as they neither move nor wear suits in contrasting colors or with bright writing on dark background.

physical properties of water, such as waves, current, visibility, etc., and much of their attitude is closely connected to these conditions. The more factors one

can recognize and understand, the more completely
one can interpret the shark's posture and thus the
intentions of the animal.

If both pectoral fins are pressed down, this indicates that the animal feels threatened. It increases its surface on both sides and enables it to escape to either side.

D (Direction)

The way in which a shark or a diver approaches clearly indicates their intentions. An animal that swims towards its goal almost directly has different intentions from an animal that approaches an object at a very wide angle. The wider the angle, the larger the closest distance at which it will pass by the human. Said simply, the more directly a shark approaches, the dicier the situation could become for the diver.

As already mentioned, one talks about the "angle of approach" when the animal approaches a human that

is motionless in the water, and of a "threatening angle"
when the human is closing the distance to the shark.
The swimming directions of a shark usually only
become obvious inside the interzone, that is, the area
between the boundaries of the outer and inner circle.
The shark does not always choose a direction that
will cause its inner circle to brush the person or
that will take it very close to the person. My experiences, however, show that—if the shark has a true
interest in the person—this will usually be the case.

The more directly a shark is swimming towards a person, the greater its interest, that is, the less its hesitation.

O (Origin)

The Origin designates the position where the shark is seen first. In some way this factor is also part of the swimming direction, if the animal appears in the normal field of vision and the person does not have to turn around. But sometimes the animal cannot be seen immediately, but only, when it is already quite close, or it may even appear from behind.

Since a shark approaches a human for a variety of reasons, and these intentions determine the manner

of approach, its position when it is first discovered is
very important. Even though science is only at the
beginning in this regard, it must be assumed that
sharks can recognize whether we can see them or not,
that is, whether we are looking in the direction from
where they come or somewhere else. How they do this,
is unclear. Depending on their intentions, they seem
to be able to intentionally approach unseen.

R (Relation)

As mentioned, there are three spatial relationships in which a shark can approach a person: at the same level, above, or below. Whichever variation is chosen indicates, just like the chosen direction, the intentions of the animal. Intentions are different if a shark is swimming at the same level as a person, from when it approaches the person from above or below, respectively from behind or from the front. A shark that swims toward a person from below sees that person as a dark shape against the lighter background of the water surface. This gives the shark an extreme advantage over the human, since the latter can barely or poorly distinguish the shark against the darker background. A shark, that swims at the same level as a person does not have this advantage. If sharks swim above a person, they accept a disadvantage— they can be seen as a dark silhouette against the bright water surface, and secondly, they themselves are barely capable of seeing the human against the dark background.

Earlier, we already discussed whether a shark is really capable of understanding its spatial disadvantage. In how far this is true must be left unanswered—but working with these animals is simpler if one assumes that they are capable. Animals that swim at the same level usually do this

while using a somewhat larger angle of approach, since they must swim around the person to avoid brushing them with their inner circle. Sharks, however, that swim above or below a person, usually keep the person outside the perimeter of their inner

Caribbean reef sharks approaching frontally.

Kelp forests are a preferred habitat of seals. Great white sharks often patrol along the edges looking for them, but never enter them.

circle (see p. 129). This allows them to approach a person at a narrower angle.

The spatial relationships can also acquire additional significance if the shark is first seen by the human in a location (Origin, see p. 140) that indicates a hidden approach.

Env (Environment)

Sharks are often influenced by the structure of their environment, such as the properties of the bodies of water in which they live and additional elements, such

as boats or divers. Therefore, at each encounter these aspects of the environment must be observed attentively and taken in. Even when sharks swim seemingly indifferently through the water, their movements are also always a result of the general environment and the specific situation of the encounter with a human, once he or she has attracted its attention. This is also true when the human does not notice any obvious environmental influences in the open water. For example, currents in the water can play a role, or the intersecting of the water surface with the inner circle. In this last situation, the escape options of the shark are greatly reduced, since the animal cannot move upwards should flight become necessary.

Furthermore, limited visibility because of cloudy water or dusk can change the shark's behavior. How much sharks are influenced by the external environment and external factors can be observed particularly well in the vicinity of a reef or other clearly structured underwater region.

Each structural element and each limitation by external factors affects the behavior of the shark. Limitations and constraints usually trigger caution or "danger-oriented restraint." The more unfamiliar a situation is for a shark, the more restrained its movements will be. The resulting behavior is not necessarily

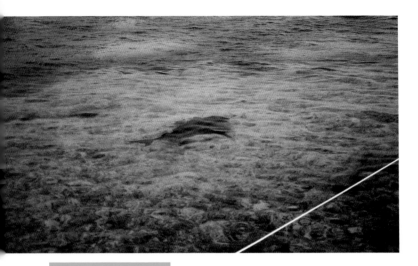

The swim pattern of a bull shark is disturbed by the shadow of a rope. Sharks are often confused by shadows. They will only approach what seems to be an object hesitatingly or not at all.

triggered by the human, but can be a reflection of the general situation.

Interestingly, sharks show a very different way of behaving when visibility is poor. Unlike commonly assumed, sharks cannot see better underwater than humans, but have to deal with the same issues as humans. If visibility is bad for us, it is also poor for the shark. In one aspect shark eyes seem to be superior to human eyes: shark eyes can better distinguish between light/dark contrasts, which gives them an advantage at dusk. This assumption is based on the fact that shark eyes have proportionally more rod cells (which are responsible for light/dark recognition) than the human eye. The ability to see contrast is a big advantage during dawn and dusk. However, if visibility is generally poor, this advantage becomes irrelevant. The animals can still hear the human, but the effectiveness of their outer and inner circle as well is strongly affected by poor visibility.

When there is such a large number of environmental factors, it can also happen that the animal only appears briefly and immediately disappears again. This is primarily observed in large sharks. Can we conclude that the shark may simply not be interested?

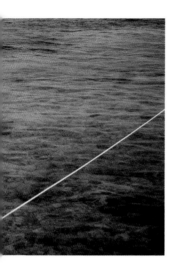

It may be the other way around—it was too interested and became unable to filter, sort, and evaluate all the external factors. What has happened here?

Sharks have a large number of sense organs (see p. 20). They continuously absorb stimuli from the environment. When the conditions are suboptimal, for example, when visibility is poor, this can trigger so many more impressions in addition to the presence of the human, that the shark cannot process all of them and moves away to reduce stress. Sharks, like all other predators, are able to focus on searching images and ignore unimportant or less important factors—but even then not too many different stimuli should influence the animal. Explanation: A "searching image" is a specific structure/pattern (for example, a specific type of prey) that is chosen from a large number of possible structures/patterns (prey animals). Other objects leave no or a very small impression on the shark, because they do not fall into the searching image. If a shark approaches—attracted by a familiar scent or sound—an unfamiliar object, such as a human, it receives a large number of new impressions instead of confirmation of the searching image, so that stress increases because the expected pattern is not found.

All external factors that influence the behavior of a shark in any possible conditions are collectively called Environment. Therefore, once again: If one interacts with a shark, it is important to observe the environment in its entirety. This is not always easy, but one can, for example, use the following checklist of questions:

- Where is the shark (position in the water, closeness to reef, structure of the environment, etc.)?

Many sharks live in coastal areas. Which species can be found depends on the type of coast.

- Are other sharks nearby that may influence the animal that is currently interacting with the person or is trying to interact with the person?
- Is the shark obviously influenced by some factor (visibility, current, and so on)?

Very often, one will know before starting the dive, which factors could play a role in the waters in question (for example, when diving along a reef, in a canal, etc.). Sometimes important hints, such as current conditions, are also pointed out during the dive briefing.

Page 150: An important factor when interacting with sharks is the current. The more aspects of a situation known before the dive with sharks begins, the more successful and satisfying the resulting encounter with these animals will be.

It is helpful to keep in mind at all times that the person is not always at the center of attention, when a shark shows a certain reaction.

   Important: ADORE is multilayered, and each diver, snorkler, and swimmer is encouraged to take and modify elements, to add new elements, and to reshape the model so that it is optimal for use for the activity in question in a specific (recurring) situation.

The following four concepts (SANE) refer exclusively to humans.

SANE

With its own activities, the human has a significant influence on the situation in question. Above, special situations have already been described, which can be elaborated on in many ways: For example, it can happen that a diver at the surface is not only drifting, but drifting directly towards a shark; or the lost weight belt drops directly on top of a shark swimming by, or drops past it; or one realizes suddenly and too late that during a dive along a reef one has cornered a shark. Many such scenarios can arise accidentally. Everything that the human (diver, snorkler, swimmer) does, and how this activity may influence interaction with the shark, is included in the Scenario.

S (Scenario)

Even though the actions of a person are in some way part of the situation, they still have to be considered separately. Depending on the movement patterns and location of the diver, swimmer, or snorkler, the situation may be more or less attractive to the shark. Each movement pattern creates sounds, and depending on the frequency and rhythm they can reinforce the situation. It makes sense that a person splashing at the surface triggers a different intent in the animal than a scuba diver who is quietly resting on a sandy

A (Activity)

bottom, photographing a snail, and not moving much. Not much is known yet about how the various human activities affect the behavior of the shark, but it seems clear that movement is attractive to sharks.

N (Nervousness) The degree of nervousness of a person affects interaction with the shark on various levels. On one hand, increasing nervousness reduces the human's ability to focus and think, on the other hand, it also increases the stress level, which in turn affects the way in which he or she moves. Nervous movements are often comparatively uncoordinated and cause changes in water pressure or noises that lead the shark to expect a juicy bite, such as an injured animal, instead of an unknown object. It must be assumed that sharks can perceive increased stress in a human in some way. How this happens, is unknown.

Exp (Experience) Even though Experience is reversely proportional to Nervousness, it must usually be considered separately.

#1: A bull shark is guided around a person…

#2: … by pushing it lightly with the hand. Even when…

In general, one can distinguish two types of experience in a shark situation. On one hand, there is the practical experience with the performed activity (for example, an experienced diver

Human-shark interaction while wearing a heart rate monitor. The heart rate acts as an indicator of the human's degree of nervousness.

versus a beginning diver); on the other hand, there is the amount of direct experience with sharks based on the number of previous encounters with them. (In this case, a marine biologist who is diving for the first time may have an advantage over a very experienced diver.)

Both types of experience can be useful: a diver who has been diving for 20 years will react less nervously when he or she suddenly loses the weight belt or drifts off. Also, in an unknown or first-time situation, the experienced diver will remain calm and react more appropriately than someone who is overall inexperienced. Experience, or the lack thereof, affects the

#3: ...sharks approach very closely, one should never hit an animal,...

#4: ... which could lead to dangerous follow-up reactions.

During an approach from the side, the great white shark is focusing on my fin. It is primarily attracted by the change in water pressure and movement of the fins.

development of the situation (Scenario) as much as the degree of nervousness.

Someone's experience with sharks must be considered in a more differentiated manner: There are people who have no or little experience with sharks in general. Others have a lot of experience with one shark species, but not with the one with which they

are currently interacting, and others are extremely familiar with many species of sharks. All these variations have an effect on the degree of nervousness of a human and they affect the situation differently. Depending on his or her experience, the interacting human may interpret certain situations correctly or wrongly and react correctly or wrongly.

Checklists for the ADORE-SANE Interaction Model

The following checklist shows which criteria should be checked off during an interaction with a shark.

Open water

1. Swimming direction (zero-<90°)
2. Spatial relationships (below, above, same level)
3. Distance (outer circle, interzone, inner circle)

Sharks often swim in large groups. It remains unknown whether they are structured.

4. Swim pattern and changes in swim patterns
5. Swimming speed
6. Orientation and position of body
7. Shortest distance

"Structured" Water

1. Position at first visual contact (next to reef, underneath boat...)
2. Effects of structures
3. Spatial relationships (below, above all, same level)
4. Swimming direction

The ADORE-SANE model is a multilayered, complex, and dynamic model, and there are a number of possible combinations. Exactly because many factors change continuously—and this also during an ongoing interaction—it is impossible always to keep track of all the factors. It is also not necessary: they can be reduced to a minimum, which is sufficient to grasp the basic configuration of a situation. During an interaction, it makes sense to limit oneself to those minimal factors. They include the direction in which the shark is swimming, the position of the animal (relationships and origin), and its attitude.

Examples from Real Life

During scuba diving some situations with sharks arise again and again. In the following sections some of these will be described, and the ADORE-SANE model applied. The emphasis is on an overall analysis of the situation, and it is assumed that the shark has a true interest in the human.

The following situations and their development are examined:

A suckerfish is attached to the lower jaw of a Caribbean reef shark. Even though sharks have many sense organs all over their bodies, this region, selected by the suckerfish, does not seem to be sensitive—not in regard to hydrodynamics either.

1. During ascent at the end of a dive a diver drifts away and sharks show up (see p. 160).
2. During a dive in open water a shark appears (see p. 162).
3. Sharks begin to swim in circles (see p. 164).
4. At dusk, an encounter with a shark takes place (see p. 165).
5. During a dive near a reef, a shark is accidentally cornered (see p. 169).

1. During Ascent at the End of a Dive, a Diver Drifts and Sharks Show up

The title describes the starting situation. In terms of ADORE, the most important factors are: Spatial Relationship (R) and Environment (Env); in regards to SANE: Situation (S), Activity (Act), and Experience (Exp).

Since the diver is directly at the surface, he or she stands out clearly from the background. As long as she does not move (swimming actively against the current), the interest of the shark is only awakened because there is an object at the surface. In this situation, the animal can only approach from below or at the same level. If the shark approaches from below the surface, one must not forget that its inner circle (see p. 129) touches the water surface and that this circumstance influences the situation because escape routes are limited and the shark cannot escape upwards.

In such a situation, the diver must take on a vertical position and allow himself or herself to drift (no movement of the fins!). In most cases, the shark will remain at a distance and circle or—if at all—only be interested in the fins, swim towards them, and in the

#1: Bull sharks in shallow water: A...

#2: ...bull shark approaches me frontally. ...

"worst case" bump or bite them. Biting must never be confused with an attack, but simply means a snapping at the fins in order to obtain more information about them.

As long as the shark does not circle within the boundaries of its inner circle (at a distance of two body lengths or less), one should continue to drift. One must not try to swim away from the shark—this is important! Should a shark approach closer (closer than the boundary of its inner circle), one can stick out a fin or a snorkel towards it and wait for it to react.

One must never forget that sharks may consider humans potentially dangerous. They do not know that we cannot suddenly bite. If the animals remain at a distance equaling the boundary of the inner circle, one can obtain additional information about their attitude and posture. Visible behaviors, such as rolling of the eyes or turning of the head (see p. 26) can be clearly distinguished and offer further indications on the situation.

#3: …It seems to realize…

#4: …that it is not the focus of my attention.

2. During a Dive in Open Water a Shark Appears

In this situation, the lack of an Environment (Env) and the Spatial Relationship (R) are the key points in regards to ADORE, while for SANE they are the Situation (S) and Activity (Act).

If one is in open water where the bottom is not visible, and also far away from the surface, a shark does not have any relationship to any features either—except to the diver. It only sees the diver and uses it as its point of reference. Because such a situation is not influenced by a reef, the bottom, the dive boat, or anything similar, the encounter is very direct. Since one is in open water, it is usually not easy to categorize the spatial relationship to the shark. One should note whether the shark is at the edge of the field of vision, and whether it is swimming noticeably above or below the person. This usually only becomes clear when an animal is inside the interzone (see p. 143). As

In rare cases a single shark appears. If one is ascending, this can lead to an unpleasant situation. The best way to handle this is to continue ascending, but minimize fin movement.

hinted in the previous example, a shark will in most cases focus on the legs of the diver and less on the center of the body. There are probably several reasons for this, but it seems that sharks primarily focus on body parts that are moving (actively or passively). The arms are moving also, but they usually do this in front of the dark background of the upper body, so that these movements are more difficult for the shark to see.

When an interaction is initiated, the human best remain passive and give the animal an opportunity to reveal its intentions. If the shark is only swimming back and forth or circling at a great distance, one can approach the animal and thus trigger reactions. In my experience, one can actively approach sharks without negatively changing the situation after the animal has performed several swimming approach patterns that did not trigger a reaction from the diver. If one wants to actively interact with the animal now, one must (!) always keep in mind its inner circle, swimming direction, and threatening angle.

3. Sharks Begin to Swim in Circles

When sharks circle divers, the concepts Origin (O), Spatial Relationship (R), and Environment (Env) of ADORE are significant, as well as Situation (S), Activity (Act), and Nervousness (N) of SANE.

If sharks are very close to a person, they were probably attracted by something specific. This may have been done consciously by the diver or swimmer, who for example, speared a fish (this sport is quite popular in the US), made significant noise with his or her equipment, or simply splashed while swimming at the surface. Whatever the trigger—when sharks begin to swim in circles, they are already interested in the situation.

First, one must immediately stop moving and take on a vertical position. If several sharks are circling a person, the person should turn in the opposite direction from the direction in which the sharks are swimming, if the animals are obviously swimming in one direction. This will keep the shark from approaching the diver or swimmer from behind (Origin). Should this happen anyway, this shark must be given top priority and be actively interacted with. This is done by either swimming towards the animal, or by extending a fin or snorkel towards it. The animal will react— usually it will increase its distance, and usually it will continue to circle at a larger perimerter.

If none of the animals approach, and there is time to analyze the situation, it is appropriate to consider all aspects of ADORE-SANE and to ask oneself, for example:

1. Is there a special aspect of the environment that may have caused the sharks to circle?
2. What is the spatial relationship of the animals to the diver? Is there a pattern?
3. Are the swim patterns changing or do they remain the same?
4. Do the animals remain in the interzone, are they approaching, or have any of them crossed the boundary of the inner circle?
5. May any behavior of the diver have triggered the circling of the sharks?

4. At Dusk an Encounter with a Shark Takes Place

Such a situation is primarily influenced by the Environment (Env) in the context of ADORE, that is, by the time of day. All other factors depend directly or indirectly on this.

Dusk means that the human cannot see the shark very well, but the shark can see the human. Sharks have a tapetum lucidum in their eyes, a layer of cells that contain a silvery pigment, and can not only see better than humans in low light conditions, but also at a higher contrast level.

If there is no lamp or other source of light available in the water, one should try to focus slightly to the side the animal to increase one's own ability to see contrast. If there is a reef or bottom nearby, one should swim there (unless the bottom is light sand). If one is already at the bottom or near a reef, and the shark is still showing increased interest, one should stop moving completely. The shark, even though its ability to see is also restricted, can still perceive the overall movement of the person. Not infrequently it will

choose to position itself in such a way that it becomes less visible against the background.

If one has an underwater light, one should never (!) shine it directly at the shark, but wave the source of light around. This waving is done in such a way that

Sharks have a greater ability than humans to distinguish contrast at dusk.

Aggregations of Caribbean reef sharks and blacktip sharks during "chumsicle" feeding.

the shark remains at the periphery of the light cone.

Most sharks react minimally or not at all to the light. However, in my experience, a shark that is very close can be blinded with a bright light. This carries the risk of an uncontrollable reaction from the animal. Shark interactions at dusk are not dangerous, but one must adapt a little by taking into consideration that one will most likely see the shark later than in daylight, and that one should probably use a somewhat different dive profile.

This situation is probably the one that arises most commonly for scuba divers. In respect to ADORE, the Environment (Env) is important, in regard to SANE the Activity (Act) of the person, Nervousness (N), and to a lesser extend also Experience (Exp). If the diver becomes aware of being confronted with a shark that is moving somewhat restlessly (Attitude (Att), which also requires experience), all movement must immediately cease, but one must make sure one is not blocking passage through or away from the reef. If the human is not inside the inner circle of the shark and thus at least more than two body lengths away from it, there is no reason for concern. In this situation, one must ask where the shark could escape and how to create that possibility, so that it can escape unhindered.

Important: Even if one lacks experience with sharks, one must not be afraid in such a situation! Even a shark that is seemingly cornered is not necessarily dangerous! Such an animal may have been in this location for a while; it may have followed something and then lost it before it was disturbed by the diver.

Whatever the human chooses to do, he or she should try to remain calm and assess the shark as well as all other options. The first thought that will come to mind for everybody is to swim backwards. But this is not always possible, since strong current or other circumstances may prevent it. In most cases, such critical situations are resolved by the shark itself. It may accelerate briefly and escape either over to the top of the reef or rush past the human. If the animal shows no reaction, one can try to swim directly towards it and trigger a reaction. A direct swimming approach forces the shark to react, and usually it will flee. In my experience, sharks—which unlike humans are able to limit their thinking to the situation at hand—will quickly determine an escape route when approached. Only in very few situations do problems develop and only when there is clearly no escape route for the shark.

One must not forget this: Sharks are used to the fact that other animals withdraw from them, not that they swim towards them.

Even though it is often claimed in books that a

cornered shark will attack, this can be considered a very rare exception. Of course, any reef shark can be cornered to the point where it will only see one way out, which is by biting. In cases where this happened, the situations were without exception (!) provoked extremely strongly by humans and did not in any way reflect normal circumstances. Sharks absolutely have the ability to recognize whether someone is cornering them intentionally or whether this is happening accidentally.

If circumstances demand that the shark be approached, this should happen as close to the bottom as possible. This creates more room for the shark to escape over the human, and its inner circle is, if at all, only violated briefly by the human. If the animal is very close, one should also hold one's breath, since breathing sounds often scare sharks.

Blacktip sharks are typically seen in the northern Bahamas.

Pages 172/173: A great white shark tries to grab a decoy. The eyes are rolled back to protect them.

Sharks as Gods and Causes of Accidents

Sharks in History

Pacific island populations considered sharks mythical and god-like animals from the beginning of time, while the Western world primarily associated them with the terms "evil" and "dangerous." This difference between people that are close to nature and so-called civilized and industrialized people is telling. So-called primitive people were much closer to animals and understood them much better. What our civilized nation must relearn over several generations, that is, interaction and closeness to animals—including sharks—was always known to these islanders.

Aristotle and Sharks

Native people often use(d) shark teeth (here from a tiger shark) to make tools and weapons.

It was Aristotle, the Greek philosopher (384–322 B.C.), who first recognized that sharks are different from fish, and he named them, along with the rays, "Selache." This designation is still used by scientists today, for example, for modern neoselachii or ancient paleoselachii. Aristotle already recognized that sharks used different reproductive methods from fish and that they do not have covered gills. The famous Greek studied sharks like nobody before him. His only wrong conclusion was in regard to how the animals eat. He wrote that sharks must turn on their back to eat. This he interpreted as "Nature's Justice," since the short time that the shark would need to turn around would give prey an opportunity to escape. In 330 B.C. Aristotle collected everything he knew in his volume *Historia Animalum*. It took over 350 years until sharks again became a topic in the writings by the older Plinyus.

Sharks—sometimes feared, sometimes deified.

Plinyus the Elder, a Roman writer (23–79 A.D.), created the name "dogfish," which he used to generally refer to sharks. The term was integrated into the English language and is used for all smaller sharks. Afterwards, the historical records become sketchy again, and there are only fragmentary notes from Plinyus and from the Middle Ages about these animals in the Western world. In Marco Polo's writings around 1298 C.E. there is a description of a ritual on Sri Lanka where pearl divers used shark charmers to protect them from sharks.

Plinyus and Marco Polo

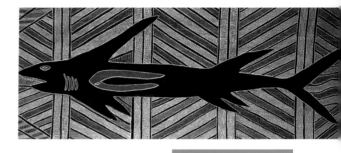

In many Pacific island cultures sharks play a very special role.

Sharks from the Point of View of Seafarers

Around 1500, the two explorers Columbus and Magellan mentioned sharks in their notes. Ferdinand, one of Columbus's sons, wrote that it is a bad omen that his father saw a shark during his passage in 1502. He believed that sharks could sense ahead of time if things would take a turn towards the worse. Magellan was obviously much more practically inclined: he only mentions that large sharks are not very palatable.

At the same time, British seafaring increased considerably and sailors often came into contact with sharks, either when fishing, or simply because sharks are among the animals one encounters on long ocean journeys, for example, when throwing trash overboard or when shipwrecked. It is interesting that the word used in English, "shark," did not have this meaning back then, but was only used for people of bad character. It is also interesting to know that the English word "shark" is derived from the German word "Schurke" (villain). So what were sharks called in English in those times? There were two names: one was the above-mentioned "dogfish," which included all

Senseless killing of a
perfect predator.

small species, the other, "tiburon," was used for large sharks. "Tiburon" was adopted from Spanish, where the shark is called *tiburon*. The name "shark" seems to have been adopted around 1560. According to historical tradition, the slave trader Sir John Hawkins is said to have brought a shark to London, and it was overheard that his people called this animal "sharke."

Shakespeare also used "shark" for the first time in his *Macbeth*, published in 1606.

Even though there were varying names for sharks around 1600, English history books show that accidents involving sharks were already known. The first truly documented shark accident was described in 1580 and took place on a trip between Portugal and India. According to reports, a sailor fell overboard and was pulled back in on a rope, at which point a shark showed up, swam towards the sailor, and tore him to pieces.

Since then, sharks have been considered dangerous, and that attitude of humans towards them has not changed to this day.

The same is also true for the supposed medicinal qualities of various shark body parts, which were "discovered" about 100 years later. In 1691, the Frenchman François Leguat, who attributed an analgesic effect on women giving birth to shark brain. And, the personal pharmacist of Ludwig XIV prescribed a daily glass of white wine mixed with two teaspoons of dried shark brain to the king. Even today, many people in Western countries incorrectly believe that shark cartilage can cure cancer.

Sharks, the Unknown Living Beings

In the Middle Ages and afterwards knowledge about species of sharks was rare: on one hand, sharks were not studied with focus, on the other hand, one also did not have a lot of access to the animals. It is therefore not surprising that the German ichthyologist and medical doctor Markus Block distinguished only 14–15 species of sharks in 1795, such as the catshark, the dogfish, and the angel shark, just to name a few. Block did, for example, not know about the whale shark, which was discovered in 1828. The next 15 years saw the first descriptions of additional species, and in Oliver Goldsmith's *History of the Earth and Animated Nature* from 1844, 30 species are described.

It is surprising that even though many of the earlier ideas, for example, about the classification and biology of sharks, have in the meantime been discarded, some of these early ideas have survived until today. How is it that after more than 400 years sharks are still seen mostly in the same (bad!) light? This is certainly to a large degree because the researchers that could have researched and described (and should have!) these animals were already subject to the same fears as the "unscientific" public. Even in this new century, there are only a handful of researchers who have abandoned this negative way of thinking in order to study the animals in their natural environment and to disseminate knowledge that reflects the facts.

Sharks as Gods

The deplorable development for sharks, which in the Western world already began in the late Middle Ages, did not take place in the Pacific area. In many island regions sharks were considered gods or reincarnated humans, and they were honored and given an untouchable status. Christianity toppled or put aside many of these gods, rituals, and ways of thinking, but in many of these regions sharks are today still treated with much respect and often humility. However, not all shark species enjoy an elevated position; many were also hunted. Only some species, such as the whitetip reef shark, were considered to have magic powers or be embodiments of other beings.

In Hawaii some sharks were considered reborn relatives and called aumakua.They were considered protecting spirits, protectors of the family, or helpers when fishing. But in Hawaii there were also the 'unihipili spirits that would judge good and evil when one died.

The best known legend about sharks in Hawaii is the one where the mother of the later king Kamehamehas wanted to eat the eyes of a 'niuhi while she was pregnant (a great white shark; a species that was not deified). So, such a shark was caught and its eyes prepared and served. The story continues by saying that the king became unusually farsighted. In other places, such as French Polynesia, shrines were built and offerings made. There the blue shark was considered a god.

A special event was hunting of the kapeta—a dogfish—by the Maoris in New Zealand. Even though they fished for other sharks all year, the kapeta could only be hunted for two days out of each year. According to historical reports, up to 1000 Maoris were sent to sea. Not only in New Zealand, but also on the Tonga Islands, priests performed rituals before the hunters went to sea.

Even though there is only a little information about this practice, it must be assumed that the so-called kanu maño priests, who through history in Hawaii were a kind of shark guardians, were the first to actively study the body language of sharks. They felt very connected to the aumakua, protective family spirits that look like sharks, and it can be assumed that they entered the water to communicate with them, that is, the spirits that inhabit the sharks.

The War against Sharks

Even though the Pacific islanders felt connected to sharks for centuries, western civilized nations cannot or will not accept that their fear of sharks is completely unnecessary.

   If one looks back to the previous century, there are five events involving sharks that will guarantee again and again that sharks will be considered monsters by the public of Western civilization. These events are from the years 1916, 1945, 1957, 1974, and 2001.

At this location on Pensacola Beach, Florida, the first shark accident of the "Summer of Sharks" occurred on July 6, 2001.

Summer of 1916

Even though shark accidents were known from before the end of the 19th century, sharks really took center stage in the hot summer of 1916. This event happened in the United States, off the coast of New Jersey. World War I was in full swing, and people went to the beaches in droves to escape from an everyday life that was overshadowed by war, and to seek out relaxation. Within 12 days four fatal shark accidents occurred in this area, which triggered mass hysteria. Many tried everything to catch the monster, and even the American president at the time, President Woodrow Wilson, was forced to act and put a bounty on the shark that was terrorizing the area. But what so clearly seemed to be one killer animal, was in truth several animals belonging to several species. They were never caught, and the hatred of these people was never placated.

The Night of July 30, 1945

Although more attention was given to shark accidents after the events described above, one-time events were never again sensationalized to this degree—until July 1945. On the night of July 30, 1945, the USS *Indianapolis*, an American warship of the American Navy, was hit by a torpedo from a Japanese submarine while heading to the Philippines, and more than 900

Senseless killing of a hammerhead; one can only wonder about the reasons.

sailors went overboard when the ship sank. Three days later a little over 300 of them were saved. The majority, everybody was convinced, had been killed by sharks. Today, it is believed that many of these sailors died from other causes. They died of the injuries that they had sustained when their ship sank. But the fear of sharks reached new heights. And while the events of 1916 faded relatively quickly in people's memories, this story became a national event that would remain in the memories of the following generations.

"Black December"

What became history in the United States in 1916 and 1945 found its parallel in South Africa 12 years later. It was called "Black December." On December 18, 1957, a victim was bitten, two days later another one, and within the following 10 days two more people were also bitten by sharks. Two of the four victims died from their injuries.

These events and other accidents, which in the meantime had occurred worldwide, caused the Ameri-

#1: As a defense against sharks, the Navy recommended...

#2: ...during WWII to slap the water ...

can Marines to create a shark expert commission in 1958, which was to develop defenses against sharks. This undertaking was doomed to failure: first of all, none of these experts was a shark behavior researcher, and nobody dared to actually enter the water and verify any fears and hypotheses. In addition, no time was "wasted" trying to understand shark behavior, but it was simply attempted to learn patterns from past accidents.

Great white sharks often have black blotches on their palate. These have not been studied. They may be scars.

Without insight into the behavior of animals, one cannot determine the causes of attacks. When this research group could not produce any results, the program was cancelled after 12 years. The key to success would have been an analysis of the body language of these animals. This approach was only tried 35 years later with the beginning of shark-human interaction research. In the years after the commission had been dissolved, no new series of shark accidents occurred, so that any interest in further research diminished. In fact, events like "Black December"

#3: .. if a shark gets too close. This has exactly the opposite…

#4: … effect. Splashing attracts sharks.

or "USS *Indianapolis*" did not reoccur—until now.

Jaws

In 1974, the movie Jaws reached the theaters—it declared the beaches of the world "unsafe" once and for all and became the seed for the fear that humans have until today.

Since the successful run of this movie, merciless shooting of sharks is demanded as soon as there is a shark incident somewhere. For example, more than 27 years later, two sad accidents happened with children in Florida, which led to the label "Summer of Sharks." The year 2001 was not particularly unusual in terms of the number of shark incidents, but the touching circumstances of these events—in one case, a 10-year-old boy sustained life-threatening injuries, and he will not be healthy for the rest of his life and will remain handicapped—made sure that the still-existing wave of hatred against sharks flared up again with full force. That in both cases humans had to be considered responsible for these accidents—in both cases, sport fishers had triggered the accident—was kept quiet and never found its way into the media.

Analysis of the 1916 Incident from the Point of View of a Shark Behavior Researcher

Each of these events that took place between 1916 and 2001 could produce enough material to fill whole books. Each of these accidents comes with innumerable question marks, and there are about as many theories on how they happened as there are people telling the story.

Here I would like to discuss the events of 1916. Even though this case is "officially" still unsolved, there are good indicators that help explain the past and eliminate many of the questions. First, I will describe this tragic summer in chronological order.

The first fatal accident happened on July 1, 1916, in Beach Haven, about 120 km (75 miles) south of New York (near Atlantic City). The 24-year-old Charles Vansant was the first victim when he was playing with his dog on the beach near the water in the late afternoon. The dog disappeared and Charles went looking for it. In the shallow shore waters he was grabbed from behind by a shark and died shortly after as a result of his injuries.

The second fatal accident happened on July 6, 1916 in Spring Lake, about 45 km (28 miles) north of Beach Haven. The victim's name was Charles Bruder, originally born in Switzerland. He went into the water with a friend at about 2:15 pm. After his friend left the water, Charles decided to swim a little farther out—alone—when he was shortly after bitten by a shark. A rescue boat went out to help him, but Charles died within minutes.

Six days later, three additional incidents took place in Matawan, a village on a small river, about 4 km (2.5 miles) away from the ocean and about 35 km (22 miles) south of Beach Haven. Two of the three victims died. The first victim was the 12-year-old Lester Stillwell who, together with a few friends, was bathing in the river when he was attacked by a shark. The immediately initiated search and rescue effort brought Arthur Smith and Stanley Fisher to the location where both dived for Lester. Shortly before Arthur wanted to exit the water, he was touched by a shark. There was no bite. Immediately afterwards, Stanley was attacked by a shark when he wanted to dive for the last time to bring the body of the boy to the surface. Stanley died as a result of this bite. About 1 km (0.7 miles) downriver, some boys, who had not heard about the attacks, were still playing in the

The movie *Jaws* lives on in Hollywood.

water. The youngest of them—Joseph Dunn—was also bitten by a shark and seriously injured, but he survived.

If all these five accidents are considered together, it looks as if a shark swam along the coast, entered the river, and attacked several victims. Two days after the last incident, 4 km (2.5 miles) away from the Matawan River delta, a great white shark who had the shin of a boy and a human rib in its stomach was caught. The case seemed closed and the murderer caught. Really?

Even though we can never be certain what really happened, there are good indications that this series of accidents was not the work of one species of shark, but two, and that these five accidents were caused by three or four different animals. If we had photographs of the bite wounds, it would be easy to determine which species and how many different individuals were involved. Since this is not the case, we must rely on descriptions of the injuries, witness statements, comparisons with more recent accidents, and known behavior patterns of different shark species from modern research on shark incidents.

The first two victims were almost certainly bitten by a great white shark. I strongly doubt that the injuries could also have been caused by a tiger shark—which was also suggested—since witnesses describe the typical attack pattern of great whites. Many accidents with great white sharks that I have studied show very similar injuries, and some of them look identical to the two first accidents of 1916—attacks from tiger sharks present with completely different injuries. The animals must have been at least 3 m (9.6 ft.) long. Based on the description of the bite injury on Charles Vansant, it cannot have been a small animal. Therefore, the shark caught on July 14 was not the one that had bitten Charles.

This raises the question, whether the same animal caused the first two accidents. This is a possibility—but why were there no further accidents with this animal? Because, had it really been one individual that started to bite people, as it is often cited in the "Rogue Theory" by Dr. V. Coppelson, the series of incidents would have continued. It seemingly continued at Matawan Creek, but these accidents were not caused by great white sharks. These two first attacks probably can be attributed to two different animals, because it is much more probable that two animals came into contact with humans once each, than one animal twice, which then stopped.

The first accident happened in shallow water (the shark approached the latter victim at chest height), the second in deeper water (about 4 m (13 ft.)). This does perhaps not seem like a big difference, but "inner circles" play an important role when these animals, whose primary sense is vision, approach (see p. 129)— and this is reflected in the injuries. In the first accident, there was also a dog involved. Even though this was never considered in any analysis known to me, the dog is also an important factor in the first accident. Perhaps, the shark saw in Charles a potential competitor for its prey, the dog, and the attack was not hesitating but strong—which is confirmed by the injury. That the animal did not bite through any human limbs shows me clearly that the shark did not intend to kill the competitor, but only to warn it.

When the second victim, who lost both lower legs, is examined, the intention of this animal was very different. It must be assumed here too, that the animal ran into the person with great force. But with great certainty, this shark did not perceive the human as a competitor (unless prey fish were very close to the victim and at the same time there were other large sharks—but there is no indication of this). Since Charles was swimming in deeper water, it must be assumed that his movements at the surface and the resulting noises attracted the shark. That the shark confused him with a turtle, I doubt, because great white sharks do not confuse the two, even though this is frequently mentioned. I suspect that the animal was forced to react quickly, since visibility was probably not very good in the receding tide, and Charles was near breaking waves, which additionally reduces visibility. Therefore, the animal chose a behavior for this particular situation that it would normally use for other comparatively large objects that swim at the water surface: it rammed the object with great force to prevent it from escaping. Since the shark realized that the object was not edible after biting it, it let it go.

The behaviors of the animals involved in these two accidents were not the same. This does not mean that it could not have been the same animal; but arguing against this is that these were the only two accidents and that the animal did not appear at additional locations near shore.

Something that also argues against it being the same animal is the distance of 45 km (27 miles) between the two accident locations. This distance could theoretically be covered in six days by a great white shark— but this species of shark is well known for often spending a longer time (days or weeks) in a limited area. Here, too, one could say that the possibility exists that the animal was migrating—but in my experience this hypothesis becomes more and more improbable, the more concessions one must make.

Independent of the above, it is probable that the first two attacks were caused by great white sharks.

On the other hand, the next three accidents in Matawan Creek involved bull sharks. Why? On one hand, the wounds could not have been made by a 3 m (9.6 ft.) long great white because the type of injury is wrong for that and on the other hand, because the probability is vanishingly small that a great white shark would enter freshwater, spend several days there, and not cause an accident until it had swum this far upriver. Therefore, when analyzing this accident, one must consider which species of shark might even be able to survive for longer periods of time in freshwater. In this case, there are no witness reports, but only the descriptions of the injuries by the treating doctor—and these suggest bull sharks. If the injuries of the three victims are studied, they suggest that this could have been the same animal. On one hand, we do see several bites all over the body (Lester Stillwell), on the other hand, single bites with significant loss of tissue (Stanley Fisher), and grabbing bites (where the shark attempts to pull the object away without biting all the way through) without much loss of tissue (Joseph Dunn).

If the whole scenario is examined, these bites fit together. The injuries of Joseph (grabbing bite) could have become those of Lester (many bites on the body), if the shark had had more time. Thus we can compare the bites on Lester and Joe with those on Stanley. Stanley's injuries resembled those of Charles Vansant in the first accident (July 6): here, too, it might be the case that the shark considered the person competition, since Stanley tried to remove the boy that the shark had caught from the water. Chronologically it is possible, that the animal—after it saw a competitor in Stanley and dealt with him—decided to swim away and look for other food. But was it really the search for food that brought the animal or animals close to the boy in the first place? I think not. I believe that the sounds made by the boy attracted the bull shark. Why the animal finally decided to move on, remains open.

The question must be asked, whether this was a single bull shark or whether it could have been several animals. In favor of several animals is that bull sharks often swim in groups. The injuries described also leave room for two different animals to be involved.

Shark Accidents

The Global Shark Attack File (GSAF) belongs to the Shark Research Institute in Princeton, New Jersey,

Reconstruction of accidents using people: Simulating accidents is extremely important in order to test for various factors that could have led up to the accident. Only real-life experiments make it possible to develop defense strategies for such situations.

U.S., and deals with shark accidents, which are investigated scientifically. Shark accidents do not just happen, but several factors have to come together for such an event to occur. Shark accident analysis is a research area with whose help most accidents can clearly lead back to certain factors.

Analysis of shark accidents is based on several sub-investigations. These are injury analysis, jaw reconstructions, profile analysis of the involved animals, as well as the actual simulation of the accident. Even though shark accidents are very rare, and the scientific investments can barely be justified from an economic point of view, the work must be continued to aquire more information. In particular, because even a minor biting accident with a shark could at any time trigger a renewed worldwide media campaign against sharks, and not only endanger much constructive work towards the protection of sharks, but destroy it.

#1: Reconstruction of…

#2: …a shark accident: …

Therefore, it is important to react immediately in case of a shark accident, investigate all aspects, and determine what triggered the attack before (!) the media, always looking for the next big story, can replay their song of the "brainless monsters."

There are only between five and seven fatal shark accidents per year, but this number suffices to stigmatize all sharks as "dangerous threats." Such a way of thinking is not only pointless but wrong. Because one thief lives in a village, does not mean that all its inhabitants are thieves. In order to save the reputation of such a village, the background stories must be investigated and presented to the public, to find out what reasons a person may have had and in what circumstances he or she may have been. And the same is true for sharks. Each single event must be examined and presented to the public in order to protect all sharks.

The most important statement that results from accident analysis is that there is no such thing as a typical shark accident. No accident resembles another one, no shark attacks in the same way as another one,

#3: ...a person stood near the shore...

#4: ... fishing.

because the same factors never come together in the same configuration. It is therefore not right when it is written that there are only three types of shark incidents: bumping, hit and run, and sneak attacks. There are considerably more types of accidents. Each incident is a unique situation and must be considered as such. The intentions of the shark, the external circumstances, and much more trigger and influence the shape of an incident and then deliver clues about how it happened.

Remember how many swim patterns, factors, and situations are described in this book, and it will be clear that there are more than three types of accidents. The interactions between shark and humans are complex, and the accidents must be examined with equal consideration. A shark accident is nothing but an interaction that ends in physical contact. Therefore, ADORE-SANE can also be used for accident analysis. The mutually influencing and dependent factors of the model also apply to shark accidents. Depending on the weight of a factor, it can acquire a larger or smaller significance and be strengthened or weakened. It is

#1: Interacting with bull sharks in shallow…

#2: … water: A bull sharks shows typical…

important that once there is an initial hypothesis about the occurrence of the accidents, the most important factors are worked out. It is mandatory that injury analysis be included in the reconstruction efforts. Again and again it has been shown that a victim describes the order of events according to his or her best knowledge and intentions, and often describes it very factually, but the actual injury contradicts this description. This should not come as a surprise; because after such a dramatic experience, most people are not able to deliver a correct description of the accident—and often they did not even see the animal. Therefore, one tries to limit such interviews to factors that can be established without doubt. In relationship to ADORE, these are only the Environment (Env), and in regard to SANE, the Activity (Act), Experience (Exp), and sometimes the external Situation (S.). All other factors are usually murky, because precise memory is missing. If the time is taken to reconstruct the injury, it is usually clear in what spatial relationship shark and human interacted, which angle of approach the shark used, and what its

#3: …circling around swim pattern and shows particular…

#4: …interest in the fins

Exploratory bite of a great white shark. Note that part of the prey is touching the palate of the shark, and that the teeth of the lower jaw are merely holding the object, not biting through it. A large number of shark accidents fall into this category.

intentions were. These things taken together deliver a clear picture of an accident and allows its reconstruction.

When I reconstruct accidents, I do this in a standardized way so that the experiment is reproducible, and it is always recorded on several cameras. In most cases, shark bite wounds are only superficial; few are life-threatening or even fatal. For the few rare fatal accidents that occur in one year, it must be remembered that the shark did not always kill the human directly, but often indirectly, for example, if a large artery was injured and the victim died of blood loss later. In the following pages the two most common types of accidents, which I call "exploratory bite" and "jostling" are briefly described. in most cases the latter does not cause injury or only minor abrasions; yet, it is listed as a shark accident in the statistics.

Exploratory Bite

These bites are characterized by a small degree of injury and show clearly that the shark only wanted to grasp the person. As the term suggests, the shark tries to bring the object in contact with its palate, since it has taste buds in that area that can provide it with further information about the object or the person. This can be compared to the behavior of small children who pick up unknown objects with their fingers and put them into their mouth in order to get more information and understand them.

Interestingly, very few victims see the shark approach, which leads to the conclusion that it approaches from behind (Origin). Exploratory bite injuries occur in two ways: as a primary bite (caused by the shark) and as a secondary injury (caused by the human). Primary injuries are caused by the sharp shark teeth. Secondary injuries can occur, because sharks do not really bite the human with exploratory bite, but only snap at it exercising little pressure with their jaws, so that an arm or leg can be pulled away. The actual injuries occur when the limb is pulled away. If such secondary injuries are present, the primary injury usually only consists of

tooth impressions that easily allow reconstruction of the orientation of the animal, the bite and swimming angle, and also the amount of pressure in the bite. If injuries are examined in this way, accidents can be reconstructed well, so that its events and trigger situation can be determined.

Preparations for an experiment: The effect of ramming by a large shark is to be studied.

Exploratory bites not only reflect a typical exploratory behavior, but are also the final step in the actual approach between a shark and an un-known object. In most cases, the shark will swim away after an exploratory bite. In this context, it is interesting to ask what motivates the shark to bite in the first place. Several factors must come together to lower a shark's inhibitions so much that

it will risk biting—it must always be kept in mind that humans are unknown objects to sharks and thus cat-egorized as dangerous, for example, because of our usually larger size than the shark. When a shark, in spite of this potential danger that we must represent, approaches anyway and maybe even bites, the trigger factors for this behavior must be quite strong.

The "innards" of a mechanical shark for studying the force and effects of bites on objects.

A good example for this is a scenario that repeats annually in Florida. Most swimmers and surfers there are bitten by a shark when they are near sport fishers. The reason: sport fishers catch fish with bait, the fish wiggle as soon as they are on the hook, lose scales, release feces and hormones into the water because they are stressed, and create all sorts of noises. These

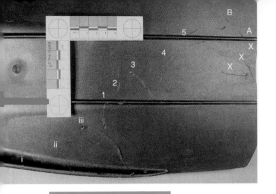

Analysis of a tooth pattern after a bite by a great white shark in the fin of a diver. The numbers 1–5 designate lateral teeth of the lower jaw, the letters i, ii, and iii label the frontal tooth marks. The most important scratches were created by teeth iii, 3, and 4. X marks a scratch from an unknown tooth. A and B are marks made by teeth 4 and 5.

sounds spread through the water, and feces or stress hormones are carried away by the current. These noises and scents, and generally the bait of the fishermen (often consisting of ground up fish parts) are noticed by sharks, which search for the source. Scent and sound waves that are between 200 and 400 Hz are the most effective ways of attracting sharks because they can be noticed at great distances. If these sharks now swim against the current, they may come into contact with surfers and swimmers that are active at the surface.

Surfers and swimmers may not look like prey, but the deciding factor for the shark, is that they smell (in reality they're only surrounded by these scents) and also sound right. Maybe some of the sounds produced by the surfers and swimmers are also similar to those of wiggling fish, that is, potential prey items.

That the person does not look familiar to the shark is not really crucial because, especially when visibility is bad, a shark must come very close to an object in order to see it. Even if the shape does not look like prey, the changes in water pressure caused by arm, leg, and general swim movements, can be read as confirmation of a prey item. Because all (!) prey animals—from the smallest fish to the greatest whale—

Piece of a boat propeller bitten off by a great white shark.

displace water when they move. And finally, movements can also be interpreted as propulsion. If the factors that trigger biting are taken together, they are scent, water pressure, and movement.

Decoys are usually only touched lightly by great white sharks. But it can happen, that a piece is bitten off.

Shark research is still in its beginning stages, but it can already be considered certain, as illustrated in the above example, that several factors must come together for accidents to happen. If we examine once more the usual exploratory bites that occur along the coast of Florida every year, we find the same factors in respect to ADORE-SANE. Referring to the shark part of the model (ADORE), the same is always true for the Environment (Env): current, shallow water, and bad visibility; and regarding the Spatial Relationships (R), the shark always approaches from below (never from the side). In regards to SANE (human centered) the Activity (Act) is always swimming or surfing, and the Situation (S) is marked by the closeness of sport fishers. If one would wish to weigh these factors, in my experience, the sport fishers and bad visibility play the largest role.

Sharks react to the noise of fish wiggling, which are often injured. Such noises can also be caused by humans.

Another way of getting to know one another is jostling. It happens for the same reasons as exploratory bites, but the object is not bitten, only touched. Little is known about this form of interaction, but it can be assumed that the shark collects similar information as with the exploratory bite. Since sharks are capable of recognizing the temperature, pressure, and maybe also surface tension of the materials they touch, it can be imagined that this form of interaction provides as much information to the shark as biting.

Jostling

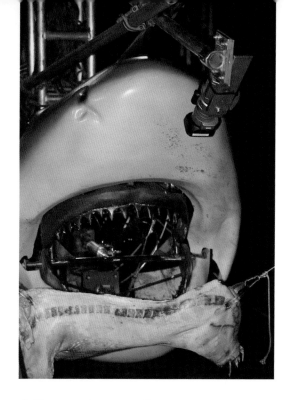

Several cameras film ramming experiments so that they can be studied in slow motion.

General Remarks on Shark Accidents

Even though exploratory bites and jostling already explain a large number of shark incidents, a few notes about shark accidents in general are presented here.

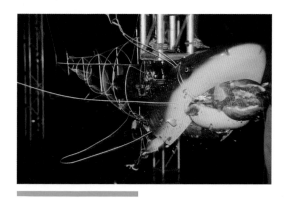

Ramming a water melon at 40 km/h.

For many readers the phrase "shark accidents" will not have the same meaning as the phrase "shark attack." This is good. The first one happens; the second is a creation of fantasy, fear, and ignorance. Sharks "attack" humans not in order to hurt them, but they bite humans when a number of factors lead up to it. In all cases, it is the human who triggers the accident—consciously or unconsciously—but never the shark. For years I have been looking for an accident that shows me even once a shark attacking for no reason or without provocation by the human. I have never heard of such an accident.

The shark reacts to a situation when it is together with a human. Unfortunately, the term "shark attack" is deeply ingrained in the human mind, so that the situation seems clear—sharks are the perpetrators, humans the victims.

In my work as chief scientist of CSAF I have pretty much seen all types of shark injuries on humans: from small scratches to the loss of body parts. What I have never seen is a single injury that made me think that the animal attacked intentionally and only to cause damage. When one has studied bite injuries for many years, one acquires not only a "feel" for the wounds, but can also quite easily imagine how it was inflicted. Even though shark attacks are publicly still presented as the great unknown, today we can determine quite precisely why an accident happened. With a few exceptions, the underlying motivations of the involved shark can easily be recognized, because each injury tells a story if one knows how to read it.

Not all injuries are the same. They are all different in size, depth, position on the body, SAP (Symphysial Axis Projection: direct line between the center of the upper and lower jaw to determine how much of a person's body was inside the mouth of the shark), and the angle of the bite, including variations caused by movement, position, weight, and size of the affected persons, as well as their reaction during the accident, to mention only a few points. Once all these factors are determined and analyzed, the most likely motive of the shark emerges. Of course,

A jaw model of a bull shark used to study its force applied to human-like tissue.

Reconstructed injury for analyzing an accident.

Measuring drag on a human when rammed by a shark during an accident.

Bite test on a
surfboard in the
laboratory.

Instrument to
measure the force of
a shark bite.

Page 199: Chain mail
to protect against
shark bites during
experiments.

there are intentions, such as "playfulness," where the injury looks more like a bite progression (that is, a bite that can change into other types of bites, and where several small bites may overlap), which makes analysis more difficult; but here interviews with the victims (if that is still possible) are helpful. The victim can of course not say whether the animal only wanted to play, but questions such as, "how did it feel," and, "what were you doing when you became aware of the bite," usually clarify the situation together with bite analysis.

In order to correctly judge the person's injuries, it is also important to be familiar with typical injuries on real prey animals (baseline). Unfortunately, these are not available in large numbers, because it presumes that a prey animal escapes the shark, and that the injury was so light that escape was possible. And then, these escaped victims must be found.

Bite patterns, injury analysis, and accident reconstruction could fill books and cannot be discussed further here. It must be noted, however, that we spend a lot of energy on investigating these few accidents every year. Even though some may consider it a waste of time, it must be said that accident analysis can make an essential contribution to shark conservation. One scratch by a shark can endanger or even destroy

all our work towards a better understanding of sharks—and thus it is important that accidents not be sensationalized but analyzed factually and explained with the facts published.

Bait is attached to pressure sensitive instruments to make them more attractive to the shark.

There are between 70 and about 100 shark accidents annually. Of these, maybe five to seven are fatal. If one considers that billions of people worldwide bathe, surf, and dive every year, these numbers are miniscule. And this is a fact: the probability of being bitten by a shark is almost 0 and should be proof enough that sharks are generally harmless.

The fear of being bitten by a shark is certainly a real feeling, even if the fear that the first available shark will come running and bite mercilessly as soon as one enters the water is completely unfounded. However, this fear should not be dismissed lightly, but taken seriously. In our work, we often come into contact with people whose fear of sharks, "selachophobia," is so extreme that their movement patterns change as soon as they enter the water, and their stress level increases to the point where aborting the dive or snorkel outing is advised.

Could such stress states attract sharks, or could sharks be aware that an object is not moving "normally"? I am completely convinced that this is so! A shark does not need to see a wiggling fish in order to find it. And stressed humans wiggle around too. Research in this area must be intensified in the coming years. Much remains to be done.

Pages 200/201: Because of their fearsome appearance, sand tiger sharks were often hunted and killed.

The Shark Success Story:
Shark Evolution

The body language of sharks is as old as sharks themselves have been on this planet. Whether the first ancient sharks of over 400 million years ago were sluggish or agile, they still had to move, feed, and reproduce. All these behaviors found their expression in body language. Of course, nobody can say exactly how early sharks approached unfamiliar objects, but it can be assumed, that this too did not happen at ramming speed, but cautiously and with a corresponding strategy.

Sharks belong to the most successful group of animals in the history of Earth. Their origin is still much in the dark. Depending on dating of the geological formations where the earliest fossils of sharks were found, their origin seems to fall between 410 and 430 million years before the appearance of humans. Except for a few fossil finds where whole animals were fossilized so that their shape was apparent, today's knowledge on the evolution of sharks is primary based on fossilized teeth and scales. Apart from bony teeth and scales, the skeleton of sharks, unlike that of bony fish (Class: Osteichytes), has no bones but only cartilage. Therefore sharks, together with rays, skates, and chimeras, are all are grouped together as cartilaginous fish (Chondrichtyes or Elasmobranchia). Cartilage fossilizes poorly and only under very special conditions, so that there are few fossil finds. The only thing that always fossilized from dead sharks were their teeth, which have such high density that they were preserved over millions of years, and shark scales—because the latter are nothing but modified teeth. Generally, it is easy to identify teeth and scales as belonging to sharks, but to determine their species is often difficult.

The evolutionary separation of bony and cartilaginous fish must have taken place much earlier than the first dated shark finds. This leads to the question: Are sharks descendants of bony fish, or do sharks and bony fish have a common ancestor? Depending on paleontological beliefs, one or the other is defended. In my

In souvenir shops, such as here in Key West, Florida, one can still buy myriads of shark jaws from a variety of species. Such stores encourage shark fishing and thus one should avoid buying from them.

opinion, the idea of a parallel development of sharks and bony fish from a common ancestor seems more likely. Because the representatives of these two groups have developed so differently and have, except for the shared habitat and gills, hardly anything in common.

There are scientists that consider sharks the most primitive types of fish with jaws, while others consider them highly developed.

The First True Sharks

A possible group from which sharks may have evolved is the class Thelodontia. This group did not have jaws, but their scales are very similar to those of early sharks. The oldest discoveries of "true" sharks were found in deposits in Mongolia, where the only indicators are scales. These scales were very similar to those of living sharks. Since neither teeth nor jaw bones were found in the vicinity of the scales, it is unclear whether these early species, such as the genera *Mongolepsis* and *Polymerolepis*, even had teeth or jaw bones. The first animal that can clearly be called a shark because of its teeth was called *Leonodus* and was found in several locations in Europe, for example, Niguella (Spain). This specie seems to be the first representative of an order (Xenacanthiformes) that played an important role at the beginning of the evolutionary history of sharks.

Sharks in the Paleozoic Era

If one looks at the actual evolution and differentiation of species of sharks, three main phases can be distinguished. The first phase was during the Paleozoic era, where a large number of species arose. On one hand, the early shark species such as *Cladoselache* and the xenacanthid sharks, which are also called paleoselachii and protoselachii, increased in numbers, on the other hand, during this era the first neoselachian sharks evolved, from which eventually those sharks evolved that we see in today's oceans. Classifying fossil finds into these groups is not always easy, because often there are only teeth, and one can only work by means of comparison.

Sharks Since the Mesozoic Era

Towards the end of the Permian period, about 220 million years ago, all paleoselachian sharks died out, and protoselachian sharks were greatly decimated in their species diversity. During the middle Mesozoic era, it was the neoselachii that spread unceasingly. In the transitional period to modern times around 65 million years ago—when the dinosaurs also died out—the last protoselachian sharks became extinct.

The Cenozoic era was typified by the development of all modern living genera and by the evolution of a clear dominance of the largest order of sharks, the gray sharks (Carcharhiniformes).

Today, about 470 species of sharks are known, which are grouped into eight orders.

Even though there used to be many different species that lived in freshwater, we only know of three or four freshwater species today. The bony fish were a lot more successful adapting to freshwater—more than 14% of all species live there.

Shark evolution has many question marks attached and fossils often pose more questions than they answer. The question regarding the ancestry of the great white shark remains disputed. That a gigantic shark, usually called *Megalodon* (of which only teeth and in a few

The tooth on the right is from an extinct *Carcharocles megalodon*, often called "megalodon." This species is not an ancestor of the great white shark (tooth on left), even though it is often called "gigantic white shark."

cases some vertebrae were found, which allows estimation of its size and weight at about 15 m (48 m) and 50 tons (100,000 pounds)) was not the ancestor of the great white shark, seems now certain. But it is unknown whether great whites may have evolved from mako sharks or some other group. Even though great whites and makos look very different today, their ancestors were probably much more closely related. More than 200 million year old teeth were found from animals that were very similar to modern lamnid sharks (Lamnidae = family to which great white sharks, mako sharks, and others belong). However, these fossils come from freshwater sediments. The similarity of a great white shark or mako shark tooth should not gloss over the fact that this tooth could also belong to a very different animal that fed in a similar way on a similar diet, and thus convergently developed similar teeth. There are no other fossilized tooth finds of possible ancestors of the great white shark from this time.

Shark Classification

CLASS: Chondrichtyes (Cartilaginous fish)
Order: Hexanchiformes (Six and seven gill sharks and frilled sharks)
Order: Squaliformes (Dogfish sharks)
    Families: Chlamyselachidae
        Hexanchidae
        Heptranchidae
        Notorynchidae
            Notorynchus cepedianus (Seven gill shark)
Order: Squaliformes (Dogfish sharks)
    Families: Echinorhinidae
        Squalidae
            Squalus spp. (Dogfish sharks)
        Centrophoridae
        Etmopteridae

Somnosidae
Oxynotidae
  Oxynotus spp. (Rough sharks)
Dalatiidae
Order: Pristiophoriformes (Saw sharks)
  Family: Pristiophoridae
    Pristiophorus spp. (Saw sharks)
Super order: Squatinomorphii
Order: Squatiniformes (Angel sharks)
  Family: Squatinidae
    Squatina spp. (Angel sharks)
Super order: Galeomorphii
Order: Heterodontiformes (Bullhead sharks)
  Family: Heterodontidae
Order: Orectolobiformes
  Families: Parascylliidae
    Brachaeluridae
    Orectolobidae
    Hemiscylliidae
    Gynglymostomatidae
      Ginglymostoma cirratum (Nurse shark)
    Stegostomatidae
    Rhinocodontidae
      Rhinocodon typus (Whale shark)
Order: Lamniformes (Mackerel sharks)
  Families: Mitsukurinidae
    Odontaspididae
      Carcharias taurus (Sand tiger shark)
    Pseudocarchariidae
    Megachasmidae
    Alopiidae
      Alopias spp. (Thresher sharks)
    Cetorhinidae
      Cetorhinus maximus (Basking shark)
    Lamnidae
      Carcharodon carcharias (Great white
        shark)
      Isurus oxyrhinchus (Mako shark)
      Lamna nasus (Porbeagle)

Order: Carcharhiniformes (Ground sharks)
    Families: Scyliorhinidae
        Scyliorhinidus spp. (Cat sharks)
    Proscylliidae
    Pseudotriakidae
    Triakidae
        Mustelus canis (Dusky smoothhound shark)
    Hemigaleidae
    Carcharhinidae
        Carcharhinus amblyrhynchos (Gray reef shark)
        Carcharhinus brevipinna (Spinner shark)
        Carcharhinus falciformis (Silky shark)
        Carcharhinus leucas (Bull shark)
        Carcharhinus longimanus (Oceanic whitetip shark)
        Carcharhinus melanopterus (Blackfin reef shark)
        Carcharhinus perezi (Caribbean reef shark)
        Carcharhinus plumbeus (Sandbar shark)
        Galeocerdo cuvier (Tiger shark)
        Glyphis gangeticus (Ganges shark)
        Negaprion brevirostris (Lemon shark)
        Prionace glauca (Blue shark)
        Triaenodon obesus (Whitetip reef shark)
    Sphyrnidae
        Sphyrna spp. (Hammerhead sharks)

Sharks Are Not Fish

It is clear that sharks and bony fish have been evolving separately for hundreds of millions of years, yet way too often sharks are called "fish." The similarities between sharks and (bony) fish are limited to their habitat and their gills as mentioned above. Their body languages are as different as their bodies. Anyone who has worked with fish knows how limited the interaction possibilities are. Most species tend to withdraw

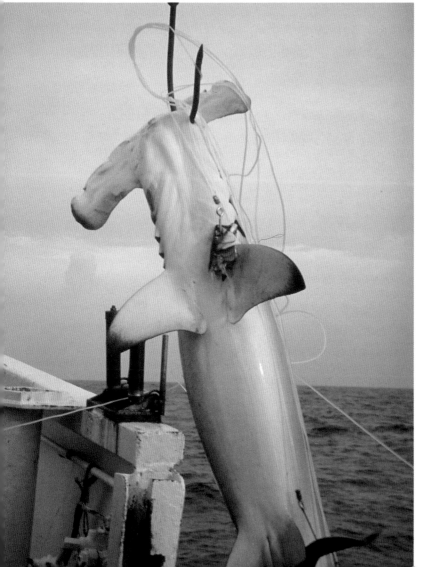

It is assumed that a shark must eat food equaling 4–5% of its body weight every day.

Dead hammerhead shark: The senseless murder of an animal that has no food value to humans.

or hide when humans appear. Species that do approach humans and are curious show such varying approach patterns that they are difficult to classify. One of the largest differences in terms of manner of swimming is that many bony fish unlike most sharks—are not required to swim forward all the time, but can stay still in the water, examine their environment, and move in place. This is accomplished with the help of swim bladders, gas-filled hollow spaces in the body, as well as very flexible pectoral fins.

Shark Reproduction

Not only must the body language of sharks become more familiar to people in order to reduce their fear, but also fundamental biological information such as reproduction should become familiar. Only then does shark conservation have a future. This section explains why. Like mammals, sharks use internal fertilization. The eggs and sperm—as in bony fish—are not simply released into the water in large amounts and fertilization left to chance, but male sharks have external sexual organs that are inserted into the female to make sure that the sperm is transmitted. Thus sharks must find a sexual partner in order to reproduce.

Gestation and Offspring

In sharks one speaks of pregnancy. It lasts between 9 and 12 months, depending on species, but in extreme cases, (such as the dogfish shark, *Squalus acanthias*) it can last for 22 months. The duration of pregnancy and size of the offspring (usually between 40 and 100 cm [16–40 in.] in length) correspond with the fact that females usually have few offspring and/or only reproduce every other year. Depending on the size of the

female, the young number between 2 and about 40 (a few species can have more young). Size and number of offspring correlate; that is, there are either many small or a few large young. Most shark species, such as blue sharks, reef sharks, or bull sharks give birth to live young. In live-bearing sharks one speaks of "placental development," which includes the formation of an umbilical cord and placenta.

Species where there is a form of prenatal cannibalism, that is cannibalism inside the mother's uterus, have visibly fewer young, usually only two to four, at most 8 to 10, per reproductive period. The number of offspring depends on whether there is embryo cannibalism (embryos feed in utero on other embryos) or there are yolk eaters (embryos eat undeveloped eggs produced later). In general, cannibalism is found in mackerel sharks, which include makos, great whites, sand tiger sharks, thresher sharks, and others.

In addition to live-bearing shark species, there are

The external sexual organs of the males are next to the ventral fins. The claspers in this picture indicate that this animal is not sexually mature, since they do not extend beyond the fins.

A helper is holding a newborn lemon shark. It is held on its back to keep it from moving.

also species of sharks that lay eggs such as cat sharks. Usually, only one egg develops per oviduct. To be laid the eggs are either pushed out or pulled out by he means of egg case tendrils. If these tendrils get caught on something in the water, the female can let her eggs be pulled out of her cloaca. If no suitable objects can be

found where these tendrils can get caught, the female is forced to leave the chosen location and find a more suitable one.

Measuring the overall length of a dogfish shark.

More advanced development is seen in species that produce eggs, do not lay them, and have the young hatch inside the body of the female. Because with this kind of development there is no direct connection between the mother and the embryos in the form of an umbilical cord, this type of development is called aplacental. This kind of development occurs, for example, in all shark species where cannibalism exists, such as great whites, mackerels, and thresher sharks.

The females of egg-laying species do not have to carry their offspring as long as the live-bearing species and the advantage is for the mother. Viviparous reproduction is advantageous for the offspring, because it means longer protection, and the young are born at a later stage of development than if they had hatched from eggs. If the offspring are further developed at birth, the death rate is lower, because they can better deal with the conditions in the ocean, and it is less likely that they will be eaten by predators.

Not only higher vertebrates, such as mammals, show changes in behavior during pregnancy, but this can also be observed in sharks. Perhaps this is only my interpretation of the observed behavior patterns, because I can tell when a female is pregnant. Unfortunately, there are no detailed studies of the behavior of pregnant versus non-pregnant sharks.

Not only pregnant animals seem to act differently, but also those that are willing to mate. Interaction of

Captured tiger shark baby, which is measured and then released.

humans with great white sharks seems to become more difficult during mating season. It is quite possible that a change in hormone levels plays a role. They are no studies about this either.

Many females seek out shallow water areas for giving birth.

Most sharks reach sexual maturity between 10 and 15 years of age, smaller species as early as 3–4 years. The latter also generally have a shorter life expectancy than their larger relatives, but this rule can be broken, for example, in dogfish sharks. These sharks are relatively small (100 to 150 cm [39–59 in.] max.) and reach sexual maturity at an age of 15 years, in exceptional cases at the age of 30 years. In addition, dogfish sharks live in schools that are gender segregated. This long period of time until sexual maturity and schooling by sexes bears the risk that because of overfishing a large number of these animals never reach sexual

Sexual Maturity and Maximum Age

Mangrove forests are among the preferred nurseries for some species of shark.

maturity, or after they reach it, they cannot find a mate if whole schools made up of one gender have been caught.

Are there correlations between body language and

state of development (newborns, young, adults)? This is an interesting question. According to my observations, the answer is yes. It is always interesting to see how sharks of the same species behave in the same situation depending on age. In general, younger (smaller) animals approach people more directly. In such cases it is important to keep in mind speed and distance: at the same speed, smaller animals always appear to be swimming faster than larger animals. Their inner circle also seems to be smaller than that of adults.

Even though sharks show very complex behaviors, have pronounced body language, and are generally intelligent, they do not really care for their young. The only care of the young is perhaps that certain species seek out sheltered locations for giving birth. Such locations are usually very shallow and thus safe from larger sharks, and have enough food available for the young. Predation by other sharks and lack of food are the greatest killers of the young. If the young sharks are not forced prematurely to venture into deeper, more exposed areas, they often remain in a relatively limited area for several years, until they reach a size that allows them to catch larger prey and stand up to larger sharks. Not all females give birth in shallow water; many will have their young in unprotected locations or even open water. The increased predation is counterbalanced by a much larger number of young.

Childhood and Care of the Young

Pages 218/219: Only in rare cases does a dorsal fin "cut through" the surface of the water. This usually happens only if the animal is feeding right below the surface.

Truth and Fiction about Sharks

"Shark Beach" of the
shark school in
Walker's Cay, Baha-
mas.

Correcting Shark Myths

Whoever studies and analyzes shark body language
intensely cannot avoid considering old ideas about
these animals and deciding that they belong to the
realm of fiction. That great white sharks confuse
surfers with seals, or that conditioned sharks bite
humans, are probably the most commonly believed
fairy tales. To investigate such questions correctly
requires knowledge of the various behaviors of sharks,
the ability to interpret simulations, and knowledge of
the baseline behavior of the animals as a basis for
comparisons.

Comparing Shark Behaviors

This baseline plays a large role when observing sharks
specifically and animals in general. Only such comparison allows drawing conclusions about whether an
animal is acting normally or differently. It is nonsensical to categorize the behavior of a shark rolling at the

bottom as abnormal without knowing what other sharks would do in the same place or situation. If 9 out of 10 sharks display the same behavior—which according to human standards may be rather unusual—then it is not unusual at all, but obviously normal. The behavior of one animal can therefore only be interpreted if it is known how this species behaves in general.

However, under some circumstances working with baselines can be abandoned: when through a succession of proofs it is made clear why an assumption about a certain shark behavior cannot be true. One must always remember that even a clear line of reasoning should be taken with a grain of salt. We humans cannot think exactly like the animal, and there is always a possibility that it could be different, even if evidence indicates otherwise.

Seals are part of the diet of adult great white sharks, while younger animals prefer to hunt fish.

Do Great White Sharks Confuse Surfers with Seals?

The above can impressively be demonstrated with the above-mentioned theory, according to which sharks confuse surfers with seals. This theory proposes that surfers and seals look the same from below and are thus both attacked by great white sharks. At first this does not sound so bad—but it does not stand up to scrutiny, because it can be interpreted in several ways.

Only surfers lying on a board have a vague similarity to seals, but not those that either sit on the board or move on the waves. But, the latter have also been attacked by great whites. Because of this, this scenario should be examined, because the shape of the surfer cannot be the trigger for these attacks. Great white sharks and seals did not meet "just yesterday," they went through some parallel evolution: one would think therefore that sharks would be familiar with shapes, sizes, and swim patterns of seals. The surfboard of an adult human is usually significantly larger than a seal, so that one must wonder whether a great white shark really would confuse such an object with a seal. Of course, the larger and heavier seals are also prey for the sharks, but they rarely stay at the surface, so that a confusion of shapes is also unlikely.

If one places something of a shape a similar to that of a seal into the water, if this thesis is correct, one would expect that a shark would consider this something a seal and attack it. However, this does not happen. We could often observe how great white sharks in such tests execute specific swim patterns—exactly those that they use for unknown objects—and try to figure out what this seal dummy could be. They obviously recognize that it is not a familiar prey item, but cannot classify it. Analyzing the shark's body language by experiments is one way to refute this and other theories.

A further possibility consists of mathematical consideration of probabilities. If the great white sharks really are confusing the two, a search and pattern should be seen. If one assumes that maybe

only every tenth animal is actually confused, and if one estimates at the same time that a great white shark eats about every seven days (most of them probably eat more frequently, even though it is often said that they can fast for up to a month), based on this assumption, statistically, every day some surfer should be attacked by a great white shark somewhere in the world. But this is not so, since only a handful of such events take place in the course of a whole year.

Accidents with great white sharks are rare, because the threshold that needs to be lowered until an "attack" takes place is significant. Great white sharks are often seen close to boats or surfers, but there is a significant motivational difference between approach and attack.

Great white sharks bite each other to establish their hierarchy.

Blacktip Reef Sharks

One species of shark, which statistically is considerably more involved in incidents with surfers, are blacktip reef sharks (*Carcharhinus limbatus*). These sharks do not eat seals or live in their vicinity, and thus the confusion scenario cannot be considered. Because blacktip reef sharks do not live in the same areas as seals and do not hunt them, nobody tries to explain why one species should have a tendency for such mix-ups, while the other one does not, when both show the same behavior pattern: like great white sharks, blacktips also use exploratory bites to investigate objects. If one reads the descriptions of such seeming mistakes, it is always clear that sharks are considered dumb animals with little intelligence.

About Shark Intelligence

Much has been written about the intelligence of sharks, but only a few experiments have been performed that allow clear conclusions. People who often encounter sharks in water, agree that these cannot be dumb animals. However, in the media they are depicted falsely far too often, and it is said that

#1: A great white sharks rolls its eyes back…

#2: …when moving from water into the air. …

sharks must be primitive animals without intelligence, solely because they evolved millions of years ago. Confirmation and proof for this assumption is also regularly published. In this category falls the expression "conditioned shark," which is often cited but always interpreted wrongly. This term usually shows up in the context of shark feeding. But what is a *conditioned* shark? There are several definitions floating around. In general, it refers to an animal that has learned to connect two events and expects or triggers the second after the first one has occurred. In the context of feeding, it refers to the fact that regularly fed sharks soon "automatically" expect food as soon as a human enters the water (the diver is the first event that is connected to the second event, the food). If there is no food, it is also said, the animals react aggressively. This reasoning has two fallacies. For one, sharks will not suddenly become aggressive when they do not see something confirmed, and second, it is assumed that one always interacts with the same individual.

#3: ...It must be assumed, that great white sharks...

#4: ... can also see well out of the water.

Shark Chumming

The above two wrong assumptions conclude that shark feeding and shark accidents with swimmers and bathers are still all thrown into one pot, and are considered confirmation of the animals' stupidity. For our studies, we often work with baited sharks. Independent of whether or not we carry food, the swim patterns of the animals and their body language in general show at most a somewhat goal-oriented behavior—but never (!) have we ended up in a situation that forced us to conclude that we would be bitten if we did not give food to the sharks.

Why a seemingly conditioned shark would not simply swim around and bite people because it expects food from them, is illustrated with some examples below.

In general, one cannot feed a shark large enough amounts (except in an aquarium) to create a dependency. A shark—of a species where this is known—requires a daily intake of food that represents 4–5% of its body weight in order to maintain bodily functions. Reef sharks that show up during shark feedings weigh 30–50 kg (66–110 lb.), so that each animal would need to get one to two or more kilograms of fish if it wanted this to be its whole diet. Bull sharks, which easily weigh three or four times as much, would needs to receive 4–10 kg (9–45 lb.) of fish. If one starts to calculate such amounts for five, ten, or more sharks, which is how many usually show up at feedings (in Walker's Cay there are often up to 100 animals)—and this every day, then this would condition 40 animals to live exclusively on feedings—it quickly becomes clear that amounts of food large enough to create a dependency could never be offered.

The "dependency theory" also assumes that each of the animals present actually eats. This is not the case.

The thesis that a conditioned shark bites humans

in different locations from where the regular feedings take place, because it also expects food there, creates a further and even larger issue with this whole story. Namely, the opponents of shark baiting assume in their chains of arguments that the sharks are stupid as well as very intelligent at the same time (!). On one hand, the limited intelligence of conditioned sharks is emphasized, which when food is not delivered, look for it from other humans and thus bite surfers or swimmers, because they are too stupid to tell a surfer and a food provider apart. On the other hand, this kind of reasoning assumes that the shark has the ability to generalize. Sharks would be able to understand that the thing inside the diving suit providing food is exactly the same as that which sits at a large distance somewhere on flat water in a swim ring and splashes.

Gaping great white shark: The slightly open mouth indicates a threatening posture.

Caribbean reef shark at the "chumsicle" in Walker's Cay, Bahamas.

On one side, one wants to prove that sharks bite humans because they are so stupid, on the other hand, sharks are presumed to have the intellectual capacity to make a connection between divers and swimmers. Obviously such reasoning is untenable.

Nevertheless, it continues to be used as proof that sharks are primitive, and chumming is a cause of shark accidents.

When is Chumming Acceptable and How Should It Be Done?

We do not want to promote every form of feeding sharks. Most of them are unacceptable, however, not because they are a "boot camp for killer sharks," but because the divers usually do not have enough positive experiences with sharks, and because the animals are usually fed in an unnatural way.

I am of the general opinion that wild animals should not be fed, but there are exceptions. Every-

thing is not always black and white; there are gray zones, and these can be well justified. For sharks there is such a gray zone when we talk about feeding them. Sharks in general have a very bad reputation. This cannot be changed if there is no opportunity to bring sharks and people closer together to allow them to interact. If sharks are not constantly fed, and the feeding takes place in a controlled environment that includes aspects of the natural behavior of the animals (feeding hierarchy, natural shyness, freedom to make decisions) feeding sharks can be a positive experience. It is self-evident that this should only be done by professionals, and each participant should be re-minded never to try this at home. Unfortunately, it happens all the time, and not only with sharks, that people overestimate their abilities, because what they observe looks playfully easy and seems easy to copy. This can quickly lead to life-threatening situations.

If an inexperienced chummer wrongly interprets the body language of an animal, he or she may panic,

Different species of sharks seem to establish a common hierarchy when they are near a source of food.

Feeding hierarchy:
Bumping and light
biting are often
observed in such
situations. These
actions serve to
establish a hierarchy.

and this can easily lead to an accident. However, such incidents are usually not attributed to the incapability of the human but the unpredictability of the shark.

Feeding by hand or with sticks has another disadvantage: The human decides which animal receives the food and thus manipulates the hierarchy among the animals. Independent of that, hand or stick feeding gives a wrong impression of the animals. The human is at the center, the shark a performing animal. Today, this is no longer a good base for interacting with sharks. Humans and animals should interact freely. That, if necessary, food is used as an aide is—as already indicated—an option and does not significantly interfere with the natural behavior, as long as certain rules are observed.

The best and most acceptable feeding method in my opinion is the so-called "simulated carrion eating" (chumsicle). Wherever animals die, sharks will show up to feed, and a hierarchy is quickly established among the animals. This hierarchy is the primary reason why feeding and divers should be spatially separated from each other. With this method, a ball of food is hung into the water, and it is left to the sharks how to feed and what hierarchies to form. Since the divers are not in the immediate area of the food, and are too far away to get into the zone of the feeding hierarchy, this method provides the highest safety margin for the human and an opportunity to watch sharks eat in a completely natural situation.

Whales (here near Dyer Island, South Africa) will often swim in the vicinity of great white sharks, but are not bothered by them.

Shark Feeding Hierarchy

Under "feeding hierarchy" one understands that sharks establish (same and different species) a ranking of who is allowed to eat when. This hierarchy must not be interpreted to mean that the animals stand in line, but that they are closest to the food, sometimes threaten each other, or push each other away from the source of food, bite, jostle, etc. Whether this hierarchy depends on size, age, or species is unknown. It is interesting that sharks seem to know exactly who is where and which animal is approaching to get its share of the food.

Around sources of food, therefore, sharks form hierarchies. Humans can also be in the vicinity of feeding sharks, if they behave properly. It is important that one does not get between the shark and the food,

The "chumsicle": A specially developed feeding method that simulates carrion eating. When sharks are fed under controlled conditions, one should not do this by hand or stick, since this will on one hand teach the shark to associate food with humans, and on the other hand, the human determines when the shark is fed. This disturbs the natural feeding hierarchy.

does not move fast, leaves the shark enough room to approach, and so on. In the following, shark hierarchies are examined more closely, because they are also especially important in situations where there is no food in the water, but the shark shows an interest in humans and interacts with them.

With its different swim patterns, the shark attempts to better categorize a human, sort of "get to know" him or her. Depending on the executed pattern, different sense organs are used, and distances to the object and escape options change. Bacause top predators are always cautious towards anything new, it can be assumed that they consider humans foremost as a potential danger, and their first approach will be patterned to leave them with enough escape routes. The humans must therefore avoid anything that the shark could interpret as a threat. As mentioned earlier, humans must not create the impression that they are potential prey by swimming away from the animal. Humans certainly do not resemble any of the usual shark prey. What is true for appearance must also be

Bull sharks investigate unknown objects by employing different swim patterns. This allows them to use all their different senses for gathering information about the object— this is also true if the "object" is a person.

Bull sharks have very small eyes. The reason for this is that they preferably keep to shallow waters where a lot of sunlight reaches the water, and thus a lot of light reaches their eyes.

applied to behavior. A shark does not only use its eyes for recognizing properties of an object. It compares the object with everything it knows and notices everything that matches. This includes movement, which is what prey animals usually do. Not only swimming away suggests something known to the shark, but also movement in place. The source of such movements is communicated through changes in water pressure. In this case, it does not matter whether the signals are caused by feet, fins, or arms.

We see again and again that especially great white sharks and bull sharks investigate fins as soon as they are moved, or they even try to bite them. Sharks can only categorize what they know, and therefore focus on what they can observe and connect with what they know, and use their own actions to discover how the unknown object reacts.

Since during an interaction one must be careful not to be classified as prey, one must be aware in which context sharks place the mere presence of an unknown object or perhaps its position. Whether sharks categorize prey into hierarchies, or whether hierarchies are strictly for intra- and interspecies relationships, is food for many discussions to come. It seems that humans are usually accepted after a thorough "inspection" and that the sharks will not swim away.

Great white sharks prefer to swim directly below the surface or directly above the bottom.

Pages 236/237: Sand tiger sharks often get very close to humans or will not swim off. This animal is pressing down its left pectoral fin and will turn away in that direction.

The "Shark School" and Questions from Divers

The "Shark Beach" in Walker's Cay is a playground for man, bull, and lemon sharks.

Divers Ask Questions about Sharks

While this book was written, the German dive magazine *Unterwasser* (*Underwater*) encouraged its readers to mail in questions about sharks. Below, those questions that were asked by the most divers and that relate to behavior will be answered.

Can Sharks Smell Human Blood?

Humans were never part of shark evolution, and they never played a role in the development of sense organs, behaviors, etc. during shark evolution. Thus, it is unlikely that sharks can identify human blood as such. It is not impossible that they can smell some components of our blood and therefore approach bleeding humans, but "recognition" of our blood can be ruled out. I know of no accident that was triggered because the involved human was bleeding (including menstruating).

Do High-Contrast Dive Suits Attract Sharks?

Sharks have good vision. Whether they recognize colors in the way we do is uncertain. But it can be assumed that they are more aware of contrasts than we are. It is often said that a "shiny" swimsuit was the reason for a bite. There are no data that support this hypothesis. The same is true for jewelry. On the other hand, first experiments with bull sharks

(*Carcharhinus leucas*) showed that these animals reacted to bright writing on dark suits. Why this may be the case is currently under investigation. Maybe the bright letters on a dark background look like open wounds on fish from a distance. When an injured fish swims around a reef, a shark may only be able to see the bright moving wound area from a greater distance. This could trigger an action pattern (a stereotypical behavior triggered by special factors).

It is a very unlikely, that human urine attracts sharks, and I know of no case where a person was bitten because they urinated.

Are Sharks Attracted by Urine?

How each species reacts to camera flashes must still be investigated. It is unclear whether they react to the light itself or to the electrical discharge. Since an electrical discharge can probably be sensed by the shark only when it is very close to the camera, the light is the more likely factor. Still, lights as they are used for video cameras during filming do not seem to affect sharks.

Do Sharks React to Camera Flashes?

I do not think that sharks recognize fear as an emotional state of humans, but I am convinced that they notice the physiological changes that go along with fear. When humans are afraid, they enter a state of alarm (stress). Their body tenses, so that their movements become less coordinated. The shark might notice that, because uncoordinated movements create noises and changes in water pressure that resemble those of an injured animal. These attract sharks. More is not known at this time, but this subject is being researched.

Can a Shark Tell When a Person Is Afraid?

What Is the First Thing to Do When a Shark Approaches and One Becomes Nervous?

Whenever one sees a shark approach and feels threatened, one should immediately assume a vertical position and completely stop moving. Most marine prey animals are horizontally oriented and immediately swim away from a shark that approaches. The vertical position of the human body and the cessation of movement are therefore two essential things that the shark does not expect. This will prevent confirmation that one may be potential prey.

Will a Shark Eventually Bite While Circling?

Circling sharks are simply interested in the situation and are not indicating any intention of biting later (see p. 42). The circling is because the animal does not want to get closer to the object (human) but needs to swim to prevent sinking, and to obtain enough oxygen through its gills. If circling sharks actually start to close in, I end this situation by swimming towards the animal in question.

Which Shark Species Is the Most Dangerous?

No shark species is dangerous per se. There are species where individuals have bitten humans, but one must not generalize from one animal to the whole species (see p. 220). Also these individual animals are not dangerous per se, because they do not always bite when they show up near a person. In a very specific situation, which is influenced by several factors in proximity to the object, their threshold for biting—and this has been shown by analyzing several shark accidents—is lowered enough that they may bite. There are only 70–100 reported shark accidents per year, of which fewer than 10% are fatal. Considering the total number of sharks and the billions of swimmers in the ocean, this small number of accidents illustrates how harmless sharks are.

If one is trained properly, one can safely snorkel with bull and lemon sharks.

"Applied" indicates that research is not just theoretical, but researchers work directly with the animals. All ideas and theories, for example, the one that sharks are attracted by blood, are "tested" on the animal, to confirm or discard them. Applied research is usually the only way to answer certain questions. I am emphasizing the word "interaction" because it is important that we also learn to understand the animal, that is, its body language.

What Is Applied Interaction Research?

In my opinion, the principal reasons for this are that one must become familiar with sharks and spend time with them in the water, and on the other hand, one must be willing to work in the field for a long time. This means that one may not be home for several months out of the year.

Why Are There so Few Researchers That Actively Study Shark/ Human Interaction?

We know very little about how sharks communicate. Much indicates that they not only use body language to interact with each other, because sharks also communicate with each other over larger distances and in

Do Sharks Have Language Like Dogs or Cats?

the dark. Even though this has not been studied in detail (I am currently working on this), it must be assumed that sharks may stay connected to each other via some kinds of "fields." This may sound like a fairy tale, but early evidence point in this direction.

Can One Help a Person Who Has Just Been Bitten by a Shark, Without Running Risk of Being Bitten Oneself?

There is no danger in helping a person that has just been bitten by a shark. Most of the time, the animal will retreat immediately after biting—and only return in the rarest cases to bite a second time. If the animal in question is a great white, it can happen that the animal remains within the field of vision. However, one may approach the injured person.

Does Feeding Sharks Change Their Behavior?

Feeding sharks only changes their behavior insofar as they are learning something new. Apart from aquariums, sharks do not depend on being fed and do not become aggressive when food is withheld. But feeding must be executed properly (see p. 226), for example, as simulated carrion eating.

Can Feeding Sharks Result in Humans on Beaches Being Bitten?

Shark feeding is not responsible for accidents along beaches (see p. 226).

What are Shark Accident Analyses and Reconstruction?

Accident research is a branch of science in shark research that tries to find out why an accident happened, what species of shark was involved, and what conclusions can be drawn to prevent further accidents in similar situations. Methods include injury analysis, interviewing victims, and investigating locations of accidents. Then the accident is reconstructed and simulated with sharks. The reactions of the sharks are caught on film, and behavior modifications for humans worked out, which should help prevent further accidents in similar situations.

Further Observations on Shark Behavior

Every time sharks and humans encounter each other, interaction occurs. There are some aspects that cannot yet be fully explained. This includes reactions of the animal that by human standards seem without reason.

I often work with large sharks in open water and look around for the animals. Frequently, I see the shark through the side panels of my mask and therefore know that the animal will approach from behind. It is thus approaching from a direction where theoretically I should not be able to see it. As soon as I turn around, or even just turn my head, the shark turns that way. It cannot see my eyes inside the mask. Why does the shark react? This fact is not really explainable, but we experience something similar daily when looking   at sharks. We cannot tell, what really happens, but clearly something did happen—the sharks see us, we see them, and something happens. One idea about what this could be—and it is already supported by some scientists—assumes that humans create with their eyes a kind of field around themselves. Then there would be a reaction between our field and that of the animal. This idea would explain many aspects of what happens between sharks and humans. New research with dogs and other animals (for example birds) already indicates that this may truly be the case. We humans also experience this, since we can sense when we are being watched.

If one studies body language and behavior of animals and humans, one must recognize that there are limits to scientifically founded explanations and accept them.

Stopping Extirpation

In the last few years, the slaughter of sharks has greatly increased. According to official estimates, one must assume that about 200 million animals are killed annually. Many of these animals are not caught specifically, but end up on boats or in nets set for other large fish. The captured sharks are never freed and let go, but simply killed and thrown into the ocean.

One of the many sharks that are senselessly killed and not used for anything further.

In many places sharks are not considered worthy of protection and are killed mercilessly. A change of attitude is necessary.

This senseless killing will have consequences: our oceans will be destroyed quickly when the density of sharks declines below a certain threshold. Sharks are at the top of the food chain and directly or indirectly control the groups of animals below, on one hand by eating enough so that their numbers do not explode; on the other hand, they keep them at optimal health by eliminating old and sick animals. Eventually, the whole food chain will collapse.

An estimated 200 million sharks are killed annually.

Many people justify animal abuse by stating that sharks and other fish cannot feel pain and therefore it is not an abuse to cut off their fins while they are alive. That is not so! All studied vertebrates have pain sensitive cells. Nobody knows exactly what kinds of sensations are triggered when these cells are excited—but in the same way one person does not know exactly how another person feels pain. Nevertheless, we assume as a matter of course that pain is unpleasant for other people. Just because sharks do not have a voice and cannot express their pain does not mean that we can deny them a sense of pain.

Do Sharks Feel Pain?

Do Sharks Have Feelings?

When one studies body language, one has a tendency to interpret movements and impressions from the animals in a human-centered way. The attribution of human feelings to animal behaviors is called anthromorphism: the bad wolf, the stupid goose, the sly fox . . . this raises two questions: Do animals have feelings? And if yes, do they feel the way we do? The latter is easy to answer: We will never know this, because we cannot put ourselves fully in the place of the animal. The first question can probably never be fully answered either. I would think that all animals have feelings, but I am of the opinion that their interpretation by humans is wrong in most cases. And as soon as one attributes certain characteristics to animals—for example, by speaking of the *aggressive* shark— one must accept that the opposite may also be correct. That is, there must also be a "friendly" shark somewhere; just as for other animals, whose simple presence makes us smile, and to whom we automatically attribute a friendly disposition.

A large portion of the sharks that are killed every year die as bycatch from long-line fishing for swordfish and tuna. They are of no use and are simply killed and thrown back into the ocean.

Bringing Sharks Closer to Humans

In any event, one of my slants is to show that sharks have everyday problems. Spectators quickly realize that even the king of predators has ordinary problems and, like other animals, must deal with the adversities of a real life.

Shark with "entourage," a swarm of bony fish that have picked this shark as their social point of reference.

It is refreshing to watch a shark that is bothered by a suckerfish and see how it tries to get rid of the pest. The most convincing example that sharks do live with everyday trouble and maybe even are bothered by them is their entourage. This refers to loose aggregations of other fish that use sharks as social points of reference. In such communities, fish larvae (such as macro larvae) surf on the "snout wave" of sharks. This is an ecological niche—a habitat—for these larva, because they often live there for several weeks. On one hand, it is an easy method for moving around without being caught by the shark (if the shark lifts its head to snap at them, the bow wash from the snout pushes the larvae out of reach of the mouth), and at the same time they are also safe from bigger fish that would normally eat them but surely will not do this right in front of the shark's mouth. Once two or three larger fish are in position behind or next to a shark—maybe to catch larvae anyway—often very quickly 20 or more other large fish join in. How much social aspects determine such accumulations is unclear. If such an entourage has accumulated around a shark, the shark cannot hunt successfully anymore, since a whole cloud of fish surrounds it like a large warning sign. The first reaction of the shark is usually unsuccessful snapping at the fish within its field of vision.

If a shark is surrounded by several bony fish, it cannot hunt successfully, since the fish will follow all its movements.

Soon the shark begins to roll on the bottom, which usually (or maybe always) has no effect.

If one has an opportunity to observe the animal further, one may witness a shark beating its head against a reef to get rid of the entourage. Once a shark reaches this state, it is certainly very stressed. If the fish are still there afterwards, the shark, apart from the possibility that the whole entourage is going to go look for a new "victim"—which usually can take quite a while—is left with only one option: if the poor entourage-tortured shark sees another shark that is

free of such unpleasantness, it approaches it and tries to sidle up to it. Once it gets close enough, it quickly moves its body towards the other shark—usually, it hits the other shark with its head—triggers a wave, and whoosh, the whole entourage gets washed onto the other shark. The first shark will then accelerate and quickly swim away.

Protecting Sharks

There are many animals on this planet that are worthy of protection, and most certainly every animal lover is convinced that his or her favorites are more important than all others. But how should species protection be decided? Is a species of butterfly more important than a species of owl? Are certain reptiles in Europe more important than certain mammals on the African continent? I think that this question about importance should be formulated differently: *Which species must be protected in order to preserve our planet—and thus us humans?* Animal conservation should not just encompass rare species, but needs to guarantee the survival of the most common ones. This does not mean that no attention should be paid to species diversity—not at all—but the priorities must be set differently. The survival or extinction of a rare species is certainly another proof of human incapability, but it will probably have little effect—

especially not on the larger ecological network, because species extinction has always been part of life and can be assimilated to a certain extent.

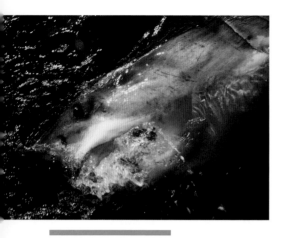

Great white shark studies a photographer on the boat above.

Species conservation has to rearrange its methods and direction, and if necessary, accept losses in terms of species diversity. With this in mind, certain shark species, such as great whites, whale sharks, or basking sharks may not be at the top of a newly arranged list of priorities. This may be dramatic for shark protectors; however, in the interest of a global view, it is unavoidable. The reason? These species have already been decimated so much that it is probably too late to save them. This is very sad—especially for me, because sharks are very close to my heart—but must be accepted. There is no choice—the main focus must no longer be on "flagship species." Shark protection must start with blue sharks (*Prionace glauca*), silky sharks (*Carcharhinus falciformis*) and all the other open ocean and continental shelf species that are killed daily by the hundreds of thousands. Because, even though the catch numbers give the illusion of high shark densities, those do not exist anymore.

Nobody knows how many sharks used to swim in the oceans before fishing started decimating them. Alarmists proclaim that 85% of this or that shark species has already disappeared. The true percentages must be significantly higher, since one can only statistically analyze what has been measured first. It will never be determined what was going on during all those years when no records were kept.

The well-known anthropologist Margaret Mead said once that one should not doubt for one second that one handful of dedicated people can change the world. I am convinced that all of us can do something for sharks. This begins by boycotting restaurants that are

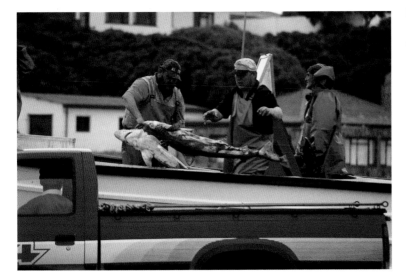

Sharks are loaded for further processing.

still serving shark fin soup, or boycotting dive areas where finning is still actively pursued.

Shark School: Walker's Cay, Bahamas

Many of the experiments and results described in this book were executed at Walker's Cay, a small beautiful island off the northern Abaco chain of the Bahamas. I do not just do experiments there, but it is also the location of the SHARKSCHOOL, a school that informs anyone who is interested in sharks on various levels. Walker's Cay offers the opportunity to get to know sharks up close and personal, and allows people to experience that sharks really are as described in this book: shy, restrained, mysterious, and everything but threatening and fearsome.

Walker's Cay used to be a pirate harbor. Pirate days are gone, but the island has lost nothing of its attractiveness: Walker's Cay is probably one of the most unique places on this planet in regard to sharks. There people can work with not just one shark species but with four or five. Whatever attracts the animals to this area remains unknown. The fact is that their density around this island is unique in the world.

In addition to the typical blacktip reef sharks and Caribbean reef sharks, Walker's Cay is the only place where one can work seasonally with bull sharks. These are the animals that have such a bad reputation, and nothing is more impressive than demonstrating in a direct encounter that there are often worlds between belief and fact. The easy access to diving and snorkeling with sharks, in concert with a comfortable island atmosphere, make this shark center very special. I know many divers and snorklers who would like to interact with sharks but are not willing to float around on the ocean for hours or even live for several days on a ship, all to perhaps see a shark. The shark school makes it possible to be at the right place in a short time, and it guarantees that one learns and experiences directly a shark approaching a person, circling, and beginning to show behavior that is seemingly "aggressive."

SHARKPROJECT

Even though a shark school is an important place for bringing these animals into direct contact with people, this close contact will always be available to only a few. This was why SHARKPROJECT was founded in Germany. This organization would like to speak to the larger public and also—unlike other shark-oriented organizations—allow everybody to actively participate. It is this active participation that makes SHARKPROJECT different from other organizations. Donors must not only experience what happens to their finances, but must also have opportunities to actively participate according to their areas of interest.

SHARKPROJECT is a hands-on organization with a small board of scientists and marketing experts, and also doctors and bankers. This makeup guarantees that a large segment of the public can be addressed, and that a variety of interests can be satisfied. SHARKPROJECT maintains a bilingual Internet site with a large shark database and information, together with forums that are accessible to everybody for exchanging ideas and information. SHARKPROJECT creates projects, from interaction behavior to advertising to documentary films about sharks. A large membership base makes it possible not only to pursue campaigns that actively lobby countries that still allow finning, but also makes it possible for more and more ideas and thoughts to be discussed, and for education to take place on a smaller and larger scale. A large number of sponsors also enables SHARKPROJECT to embark on projects that would be unthinkable for other organizations.

"If sharks die, the sea dies" is the motto of SHARKPROJECT. The ocean needs sharks, and humans need sharks. Without sharks the oceans will be destroyed. We hope that similar organizations will be created to protect all the other species of animals that urgently need our help.

Increasing understanding of sharks helps protect them better.

Bibliography

Allen, C. and M. Bekoff. *Species of Mind*. MIT Press: Cambridge, Massachusetts and London, 1999.

Bateson, P. and P. Klopfer, eds. *Perspectives in Ethology*. vol. 2. Plenum Press: New York and London, 1976.

Bekoff, M. *Minding Animals*. Oxford University Press: Oxford, 2002.

———— *The Smile of a Dolphin*. Discovery Books: 2000.

———— and J. Byers, eds. *Animal Play: Evolutionary, Comparative and Ecological Perspectives*. Cambridge University Press: 1998.

———— and D. Jamieson, eds. *Readings in Animal Cognition*. MIT Press: Cambridge, Massachusetts and London, 1996.

Bradbury, J. and S. Vehrencamp. *Principles of Animal Communication*. Sinauer Associates Publishers: Sunderland Massachusetts, 1998.

Brunky, D. B. Animal Voices. Bear and Company: Rochester, 2002.

Burghardt, G. and M. Bekoff, eds. *The Development of Behavior*. Garland STPM Press: New York and London, 1978.

Compagno, L. *Sharks of the World*. vol. 2. FAO: Rome, 2001.

Coren, S. *How to Speak Dog*. Simon and Schuster: New York, 2000.

Coppleson, V. *Shark Attack*. Angus and Robertson Publishers: Australia, 1958.

Dawkins, M. *Through Our Eyes Only?* Oxford University Press: Oxford, 1998.

Dawkins, M. *Unravelling Animal Behaviour*. Longman: Essex, England, 1986.

Dozier, R. *Fear Itself*. St. Martin's Press: New York, 1998.

Dukas, R., ed. *Cognitive Ecology*. University of Chicago Press: Chicago and London, 1998.

Earle, S. *Sea Change*. G. P. Putman's Sons: New York, 1995.

Fagan, R. *Animal Play Behavior*. University Press: Oxford, 1981.

Fedigan, L. *Primate Paradigms*. University of Chicago Press: Chicago and London, 1982.

Fernicola, R. *Twelve Days of Terror*. Lyon Press: Guilford, 2001.

Fossey, D. *Gorillas in the Mist*. Houghton Mifflin Company: Boston and New York, 1983.

Frohoff, T. and B. Peterson, eds. *Between Species*. Sierra Club Books: San Francisco, 2003.

Godin, J.-G., ed. *Behavioural Ecology of Teleost Fishes*. Oxford University Press: Oxford, 1997.

Goodall, J. and M. Bekoff. *The Ten Thrusts*. HarperCollins: 2002.

Griffin, D. *Animal Minds*. University of Chicago Press: Chicago and London, 1992.

Griffin, D. *Animal Thinking*. Harvard University Press: Cambridge, Massachusetts and London, 1984.

Halliday, T. and P. Slater, eds. *Animal Behaviour*. vol. 1. Causes and Effects. Freeman and Company: New York and San Francisco, 1983.

Hamlett, W., ed. *Sharks, Skates, and Rays*. Johns Hopkins University Press: Baltimore, 1999.

Hauser, M. and M. Konishi, eds. *The Design of Animal Communication*. MIT Press: Cambridge, Massachusetts and London, 1999.

Kapoor, B. and T. Hara, eds. *Sensory Biology of Jawed Fishes*. Science Publishers: Enfield, 2001.

Klimley, P. and D. Ainley, eds. *Great White Sharks*. Academic Press: 1996.

Lorenz, K. *Das sogenannte Böse*. DTV; Munich, 1963.

Manning, A. and M. Dawkins. *An Introduction to Animal Behaviour*. Cambridge University Press: 1998.

Mitchell, R., N. Thompson and L. Miles. *Anthropomorphism, Anecdotes and Animals*. State University of New York Press: Albany, 1997.

Moynihan, M. *The Social Regulation of Competition and Aggression in Animals*. Smithsonian Institution Press: Washington and London, 1998.

Myers, A. *Communicating with Animals*. Contemporary Books: Chicago, 1997.

Nollman, J. *The Man Who Talks to Whales*. Sentient Publications: Boulder, 2002.

O'Barry, R. *Behind the Dolphin Smile*. Algonquin: Chapel Hill, 1989.

Page, G. *Inside the Animal Mind*. Doubleday: New York, 1999.

Pitcher, T. *Behaviour of Teleost Fishes*. Chapman and Hall: London, 1986.

Ritter, E. *Über die Körpersprache von Haien*. Steinert-Verlag: Witten, 2002.

Ritter, E. *Das Lächeln der Haie*. Steinert-Verlag: Witten, 2001.

Roberts, W. *Principles of Animal Cognition*. McGraw-Hill: 1998.

Schaller, G. *The Serengeti Lion: A Study of Predator-Prey Relationships*. University of Chicago Press: Chicago, 1972.

Sebeok, T. *How Animals Communicate*. Indiana University Press: Bloomington and London, 1977.

Sheldrake, R. *The Sense of Being Stared At*. Crown Publishers: New York, 2003.

———. *Dogs That Know When Their Owners Are Coming Home*. Three Rivers Press: New York, 1999.

Shettleworth, S. *Cognition, Evolution and Behavior*. Oxford University Press: Oxford, 1998.

Smith, J. *The Behavior of Communicating*. Harvard University Press: Cambridge, Massachusetts and London, 1977.

Smith, P. *Animal Talk*. Beyond Words Publishing: Hillsboro, Oregon, 1999.

Solisti, K. and M. Tobias, eds. *Ich spürte die Seele der Tiere*. Kosmos-Verlag: Stuttgart, 2003.

Stanton, D. *In Harm's Way*. Henry Holt: New York, 2001.

Taylor, L. *Sharks of Hawai'i*. University of Hawaii Press: Honolulu, 1993.

Taylor, S. *Souls in the Sea*. Frog: Berkley, California, 2003.

Wallett, T. *Shark Attack*. Macdonald Purnell: Transvaal, 1986.

Wilson, E. *Sociobiology*. Harvard University Press: Cambridge, Massachusetts and London, 1975.

Index

Figure Sources

All photos by Dr. Erich Ritter, with exception of:
Harald Bänsch (p. 174, both, 175), Tom Campbell
(p. 119), Franz Hajek (p. 4/5, 156/157, 162/163),
Andreas Serec (p. 41, 118, 136/137, 232, 238), Gerhard
Wegner (p. 203, 245 below) and Andre Winkler
(p. vi all, vii all, 1/2, 18/19, 64/65, 86/87, 112/113,
172/173, 200/201, 218/219, 236/237).

The drawings are by Christine Staacks.

The photographs of sequences, e.g., on pages 24/25,
32/33, etc. (blue font), are taken from video recordings
of scientific experiments by Dr. Ritter, which is why
their quality does not match the quality of the other
photographs.

STOP FINNING!

SH RK PROJECT
Internationale Initiative zum Schutz und zur Erforschung der Haie e.V.

www.sharkproject.com